FROM SINKING SAND. . .

by **Marsha Lenski**

Xulon PRESS

Library of Congress Control Number: 2002100976
ISBN 1-591600-05-7

Xulon Press
11350 Random Hills Road
Suite 800
Fairfax, VA 22030
(703) 279-6511
XulonPress.com

This book is lovingly dedicated to the

glory of God, the precious family He

has lent me, and to Cindy Sue, Karen and Dave.

mll

TABLE OF CONTENTS

The only real names used in this manuscript are those of myself, my husband John and my children. M.L.L.

"Everyone who hears my words and obeys them is like a wise man who built his house on a rock. It rained hard, the floods came, and the winds blew and hit the house. But it did not fall, because it was built on a rock.

Everyone who hears my words and does not obey them is like a foolish man who built his house on sand. It rained hard, the floods came, and the winds blew and hit that house, and it fell with a big crash."

Matthew 7:24-27

FOREWORD

Marsha Lenski's story is not an unusual one. What is unusual is that she chose to be transparent enough to expose it. I'm sure it was not comfortable for her to reveal the error of her ways, but she did so that some may be warned and others restored.

The church world may bury its head when one of the flock goes astray, or they may condemn the fallen saint to isolation. Only those who truly know the mercy and forgiveness of God can be that minister of reconciliation who loves others back into fellowship with God.

I believe many people who read this story will say, "But for the grace of God, there is my life?" Those who have been down the same road will cast no stones. I trust that those who have not been down this road will see the message of God's mercy and come to a greater understanding of the enemy's plan to destroy human lives.

ANNETTE CAPPS
Life Fellowship Ministries
Tulsa, Oklahoma

Chapter 1

MRS. WONDERFUL

Old-fashioned. That would be me.

Early afternoon of a late spring day when I was twenty-nine, our new son was nursing as he and I sat together in a quiet and shady portion of the yard of our lovely home. Our daughter, Lyndsay, was two and had just succumbed to her nap time with sweet night-night kisses and "Love, Mommie, love." The part of me that had grown up longing for mother-hood, a home of my own and a quiet life was feeling very satisfied at that moment.

As I recall that day, I was so thankful that I had been blessed even beyond my wishes and hopes. God had been so good. Since I had met Jesus Christ personally and committed myself to Him five years prior, I had seen Him raise me up from some deep pits of life to enjoy with Him His promises of abundance. My life was the envy of any woman with those wonderful old-fashioned ideals and dreams. And God had put me in His service doing something I enjoyed with all my heart. Too bad I was blindly misusing it. He was about to deal with me.

I looked into the deep blue eyes of my three-month-old son. A sense of love and new commitment flooded through me as I closed my eyes and thanked God again for giving me so many desires of my heart. But one remaining area of my life with which I was unable to deal successfully was quickly discarded from my thoughts as the phone rang, pulling me from my solitude.

"Marsha, we need to meet tomorrow to discuss the special feature for next month's meeting." It was Sandy, the chairman of our Christian Women's Club, for which I served as an advisor. "I just got a call from the woman who has committed to the presentation on corn husk dolls, and she has a change in plans. Before we go to print with the invitations, we need to prayerfully consider someone else. Any ideas?"

I loved our club. I was pleased to be called to serve there. I was so pleased that I began loving the attention it brought me and I didn't realize it. My gifts had been used so well in that capacity that it was known in the group, which served 200 women, that to call Marsha meant to get the job done. I wasn't one for saying no, and I was soon to learn that someone was on to my motives, about to question them and shake me off my precious pedestal.

From the day I realized my need for Jesus and His forgiveness and had joyfully committed myself to Him, He had set my life in a new and positive direction. Many areas of my life had been changed for the better as I yielded to His divine will. However, two strongholds stayed in my heart's closet, and I was unaware of the strength with which they controlled me.

From those memorable days of young motherhood until then, life was abundant. The Christian Women's Club had become more and more a part of my life. For nearly three years a small group of beautiful women in the Lord met in my home weekly to learn and grow together spiritually. We worked and prayed together, we laughed and cried together, and we knew a bonding that was matchless. I will always remember and be grateful for those women and the fulfilling times we all spent together. Fortunately, or unfortunately for me, the studies we used were provided by a participating ministry and came with a comprehensive leader's guide. It was easy to lead the group, and as time went on I became lax in the amount of time I spent preparing to lead the study. Because of my inability to deal with the secret areas of my life, my relationship with God slowly began to deteriorate. Superficially, I was a spiritual leader in my community. In reality, I was losing a battle with Satan that I cannot describe. The enemy knows where our greatest weaknesses lie, and his attack on my life was great.

> *"Control yourselves and be careful! The devil, your enemy, goes around like a roaring lion looking for someone to eat."*
> I Peter 5:8

His claws began to sink slowly into my flesh.

Early that year our Christian Women's Club began to undergo a change. It was time to call new officers and take new responsibilities. I had prided myself for so long on how well the women responded to me and on how efficient I was that I had lost sight of the Giver of these gifts. Each time we had our luncheon meeting, I was deeply touched by the stories of women who had found God's love in desperate moments of life. My gratitude for what Jesus had done for me in dying on the cross was real and never ceased to move me to tears. What I didn't realize was that I was not allowing His love to dwell deep enough within me to fully practice what I was being taught of obedience. I still held the reigns to my life. I still thrived on the acceptance of man. Rejection was something I couldn't handle and didn't want to face.

I wanted very much to be the chairman of that club. For some reason, however, I was not being supported by the other advisors. I began to manipulate the situation. In prayer

I would tell the Lord exactly what He should do. I was the best person qualified for the job. What was wrong, then?

I will never forget the phone call. Another club advisor, a woman with whom I had what I claimed was a 'personality conflict', got the courage one day to be honest enough to tell me why she could not support me as chairman of the club. Tension was high between us. I always thought she lacked tact and diplomacy and had even asked the Lord to love her through me because I was unable to do so myself. The other advisors seemed to favor her for the chairmanship. Jealousy reared its ugly head. At that point, however, I thought I was the only one who knew it.

"Marsha," she said honestly. "I just cannot support you as chairman; I feel you are just too much of a 'yes' person." She began to elaborate. I didn't want to hear more or let her know I was crying. Fight or flight? Instead of confronting the situation in love and acknowledging her courage in coming to me that way, I chose to deny and to run. I hung up the phone. Then I cried.

"No, Lord! No, no, no!" Hadn't I been faithful in service? Wasn't I loved by the other women? Hadn't I accomplished a great deal for the club? What gave her the right to burst my pretty bubble with her lies about me? She was just jealous! And rightly so. She certainly wasn't anything to rave about!

One of my secrets had been found out. . .a secret even I had denied to myself until then. I was glorifying myself in my service to God, and the price for that is always too high. I was devastated. I refused to believe it. Because of my denial, I could not pray. Because of my shame, I could not ask for forgiveness—either of her or of the Lord. I was Mrs. Wonderful and I didn't want the masquerade to end.

Satan could have a field day with me. His laughter would soon be heard from one end of my world to the other.

Chapter 2

WHERE IS LOVE?

Are you anything like me when it comes to your children? Don't you believe your children are the most beautiful and most wonderful God ever put on this earth? I think mine are. I thought then that I didn't care what the sacrifice—I loved being a mother. I am more committed to it today, however, than I once was. My motherhood and my Christian commitment were about to undergo a severe testing, and the result is one with which I will be living for the rest of my life.

Lyndsay and Joshua could not have a better daddy. Ron is totally committed to them. He was committed to the Lord, too, and I was so excited the day he gave his life to Christ. Each of those precious babies had been lovingly dedicated as well, and we meant to keep our promise to raise them in a home where God came first. Sadly, however, we did not allow God His rightful place in our family. We served Him only in a convenient atmosphere of Christian fellowship where our superficial front was our only support. We were building our foundation on sinking sand.

The year Ron and I celebrated our sixth wedding anniversary we were both admitting that we were simply tolerating each other. My involvement in the community and with projects I felt 'led' to pursue, coupled with caring for the children, had captured all my attention. I loved having things

5

to occupy me and keep my mind off my failing marriage. Ron had climbed the corporate ladder very quickly and was committed to his career. He traveled fifty percent of our married life. He did all he could to maintain his relationship with his children, but he and I shared less and less as time went by.

Resentment began to eat away at the fibers of our life together. I resented his work and his traveling. He resented the fact that I was serving God in more ways than he was, and I even suspected that he questioned my integrity and motives in doing so. Before long I began to appreciate his absence so I would not have to deal with our deteriorating relationship. Looking back, it was me, my attitude and my lack of faith, that I didn't respect. It wasn't really Ron. But he became a convenient outlet to avoid facing the disintegration of my own self-respect. I did not want to think I could possibly be the problem. What a relief to make him the problem instead!

Before long we both began to find fault in even the smallest and the simplest things the other might do. Finances were adequate but limited and tempers flared over making ends meet. Our passion for each other dwindled to nothing but a laughing matter. Gradually, even little Lyndsay was aware that we did not get along. So we would temporarily cool it, subdue it, push it into the closet, but we would not deal with it. We did not try to save our relationship. Perhaps we never admitted how sadly pathetic it was. Another classic case of not allowing God's love to penetrate deeply enough into our lives to trust in His abilities rather than our inabilities. Service to Him? Yes. Obedience? No. We still depended too much on ourselves.

Why we did not seek God's help together is beyond me. I guess things had gone too far and the sin had become too comfortable.

> *"When people's thinking is controlled by the sinful self, they are against God, because they refuse to obey God's law and really are not even able to obey God's law."*
> Romans 8:7

We attended church together and even a couple's Bible study which we organized and held in our home. To the world I'm sure we appeared to be quite the ideal (dare I say spiritual?) couple. We particularly managed to fool ourselves more than anyone else. From the inside, however, we were sad and lonely people quickly losing respect for one another. His work and my projects were our copouts. They were great escapes from the fact that we had serious problems.

Our pastor was a fine and genuinely kind man, but he was so very busy. Our church struggled in its growth and he was overworked. I visited with him once, but he seemed to be nervously preoccupied as I poured out my heart to him. He said he would help me persuade Ron to counsel together, but I never heard from him again.

I took great relief from the fact that Ron was so close to the children. He is a good disciplinarian and always did his best for them. He's immensely proud of them. I remember at times wishing he cared as much for me. His temper never flared at them—only at me. He was not unjustified, either. I was not the wife I should have been. I began to dislike him to the point that I felt he deserved it anyway.

Oftentimes I would try to tell myself we didn't have problems. I tried to convince myself that I was imagining things. There was even a time when I felt that somehow my service to God would operate like osmosis and substitute for a deeper relationship with Him, and my problems would disappear POOF as long as I stayed involved and gave it time.

Ron had an area in his own life with which he had never dealt because, like me, he was comfortable. It was a problem with which I had never been faced and felt totally inadequate to do anything about. It bewildered me and it terrified me. Fortunately, it wasn't frequent, but when Ron couldn't say no for fear of what his professional constituents (or whomever) might think, I was the one who paid the price. I came to learn that when it happened to some people they got happy, even funny. When it happened to Ron, he got violent—the out-of-control type. The day after each of these incidences was as bad as the terror I felt going through them. We didn't talk to each other about it. I was called a liar because he would always tell me he would never have done such a thing.

It was time for love to take over. It was time to reach out to each other. It was time to help each other. It was time to trust God.

> *"Come near to God and God will come near to you."*
> James 4:8

We just never did, and the devil's claws began to draw blood. By this time, the mire into which we were sinking was so close to suffocating us that I felt God wouldn't help. The truth was that He couldn't. We wouldn't let Him.

Chapter 3

TOYING WITH DECEPTION

The 'perfect' couple got a perfect opportunity for what the world might call a dream-come-true in autumn that year. Have you ever wanted to see the world? I never thought I would have the chance to travel outside the continental United States, not until it became a reality for us that fall when I was thirty-one.

Ron had been hoping for a prestigious career opportunity overseas for years. The company for whom he had been working early in our married life had offered him a position as Director of Employee Relations at their job-site in Saudi Arabia. Saudi Arabia! I was genuinely thrilled for him, and I knew how proud he was and how much this meant to him. We began to make plans to travel and travel and travel some more. It meant we could become financially independent! It meant wonderful educational opportunities for Lyndsay and Joshua. We had something else at which to focus our attention. Our problems were neatly and discreetly shoved under a rug. . .again. We began to tell our friends and neighbors and stray dogs that we were going to see the world! I don't think anything alive and breathing within a hundred miles of us did not know how excited we were.

It was at this point that I began to withdraw from Christian

Women's Club. I still could not face the secrets I had been living by and was ashamed that my integrity had been questioned. More importantly, I still could not face God with the sad relationship I called a marriage. Shame and guilt kept me from Him. I used our relocation to Saudi as an escape hatch and apologized to the club for the fact that preparations would soon keep me too busy to participate. Such was not the case. It took three months to process Ron out of the country, and I would not be able to join him for at least three months beyond that. My deception went deeper still. I even started believing that this might be what could repair our unhappy marriage.

There were tears in the good-byes to my friends from Christian Women's Club. . .friends with whom I had truly seen the love of God magnified. Apparently my 'enemy' (who knew the truth about me) had been kind enough not to gossip. No one else knew what she and I knew. Today I am sure her heart was broken as she watched me leave the service of that wonderful group of women. She had loved me enough to be honest with me and perhaps sensed the hurt in my life. But I had backed off so abruptly that I could not be reached, even with the kindest thoughts.

God tells us in II Corinthians 11:14:

> *"Even Satan changes himself to look like*
> *an angel of light."*

He knows exactly where our greatest weaknesses lie, and if he can manage to deceive a leader in the Christian community, his victory is all the sweeter. By this time he must have been well aware that the battle for my life could likely be his. He moved in for the kill, wringing his hands with delight, no doubt. I didn't recognize his tactics then. Today I know it was at this point that I succumbed to his oppression and opened wide the door to temptation. He dangled an apple in front of me and I was too weak to resist. He made it look so good. Oh, it looked so good! And he made it look harmless. No one would know. My weakness was about to be preyed upon, and when he gained this stronghold, he painted such a rosy picture that I was blinded and saw absolutely no wrong in what I was about to do. God, forgive me, I saw no wrong.

Ron left for Saudi Arabia in October, six days after our sixth wedding anniversary. I'll never forget the moment he boarded that plane. As they began to call the passengers I remember holding him tighter than I ever had. Even though I was fully aware of what I had been planning and was about to do, my conscience told me to cling to my husband. The battle raged inside me. I said "don't leave me", and my eyes brimmed with burning tears. Neither of us realized at that moment that it was the beginning of a sad and lonely end for us.

Ron left with hope in his heart, looking positively toward the future. He had no idea what was happening inside me. He only passed it off as my normally emotional nature.

On the drive home, some thirty miles, the demon which had captured my spirit with the false excitement of the opportunity that would soon be mine recaptured my thoughts and regained his hold on my heart. Now I was alone to plan a rendezvous that would blow the roof right off my world. But I could not resist.

Chapter 4

A WAY THAT SEEMED RIGHT

Even as Christians we have a choice of will in all circumstances with which we are confronted. God desires that we make the right choices in obedience to Him. He always knows what lies ahead, and the consequences if we should choose the wrong path. His Word says:

> *"A thief comes to steal and kill and destroy, but I came to give life — life in all its fullness."*
> John 10:10

The choice remains our own.

Once the choice is made to sin (…*"Anything that is done without believing it is right is a sin…"* Romans 14:23b*)*, the enemy has a sadistic way of making the road appear paved with gold. It's easy for him once our choice is made. At this particular time in my life it not only looked easy but it seemed right for me, right for my life at that time.

> *"Some people think they are doing right, but in the end it leads to death."*
> Proverbs 16:25

Rather than seeking to help my husband and to work to repair my failing marriage, I secretly and selfishly felt it was time for a change, that I owed it to myself and deserved it as well. I blamed Ron and our marriage for leaving me empty and unsatisfied with no self-respect or self-worth. What a great deception I was accepting for truth at the time. Now that the temptation had me, Satan was going to make sure that everything important to me fell under his dictatorship. The better he could make it all look the more complete my destruction. He attacked the most vulnerable area to me at that time: lust—lust for life, lust for attention and sexual lust. Oh, how I longed to be valuable to someone again—a man—a man whose attentions could reaffirm that I still 'had what it takes', that I was still beautiful and desirable. I believed it would take another man to fill the void left by my less than perfect marriage. My worth came from the world, from people, from a person. I was so dependent. Sadly, it wasn't only the wrong way out I chose. It was the coward's way out. I waited until my husband left the country. . .it would make everything easier. By this time I cared for nothing more than meeting my selfish needs.

Within two weeks of Ron's overseas departure I had arranged for Lyndsay and Joshua to stay with a trusted friend and I was on a non-stop flight from Chicago O'Hare to my old playground: glamorous San Francisco, leaving behind me a path of lies and deception from here to eternity. I didn't care anymore, yet the person I deceived the most, unfortunately, was myself. Besides, this was just a temporary thing, just a fling to satisfy some small need. No one would ever be the wiser. No one was going to get hurt. No one would even have to know. As far as Ron was concerned, he and I had agreed that he would not phone me until a certain date, which gave me plenty of time to accomplish my goal and return home without putting a dent or ripple in our family relationship.

As I stepped off that plane I picked him out in the crowd

immediately. Craig. There he was, as handsome as I remembered from seven years before. His smile was broad, genuine and reassuring. He had a longing in his eyes that I knew well. The first tugs at my heartstrings put me on full alert, and there would be many more. It's called false hope. But that's not what I saw at the time. The rest of the world seemed to vanish as he took me in his arms and we became lost in our own world.

Before I met Ron, he had been my one great love. But because of our age difference (he is considerably older than I), I had chosen to break off our exciting relationship to pursue another. Over the years I heard about him through the grapevine. He had never married. When I called him long distance prior to my arrival, I wondered with a trembling hand on the telephone whether he would even remember me. Satan was way ahead of me and used Craig superbly to set the stage. Not only did Craig remember me but immediately recognized my voice even after all the years. He didn't know God and was not bound by any heavenly obligations. He was a perfect instrument by which the enemy could accomplish his purpose. Craig was delighted that my husband was leaving town and he could have a chance to see me again! As I said, once the choice is made to sin, the enemy has a way of making the road look paved with gold.

For several days we laughed, we reminisced, we loved and we toyed with our lives. I was ecstatic! I'd never had so much attention, so much of everything lavished on me. I'd never dined so elegantly, dressed so beautifully or tossed such caution to the wind.

> ". . .foolish plans are like planting the wind,
> but they will harvest a storm."
> Hosea 8:7

I knew Craig was professionally a very successful man. What I didn't know was to what extent he took this success, how much wealth he really had and to what degree it possessed him. I was too busy to give thought to what materialism had done to his mind. There he was when I needed him—and I needed attention the way he gave it to me. I basked so thoroughly in false hope and superficial values that I didn't see that side of him. I avoided looking at it, denied it. He was sincere and generous—that's all I saw. I was having the time of my life! The more he fed my deteriorated self-worth and ego, the more I got lost in how good it felt. This very eligible San Francisco bachelor wanted me and did his best to please me—of all women! Nobody was going to take him from me. The more time I spent with him, the deeper I sank into the mire of deception and the better it looked to me. Before long, I became possessive of him and vowed that no one, not God, not Ron, not my children—no one was going to spoil this for me. Me! Me!

One day during my stay in California, when I happened to be alone, the phone rang unexpectedly. Satan knew he had me cornered and was about to prove it. My thoughts went to my dear friend who had my children and this number in case she needed me. I checked on the children more than daily and would soon be returning home. Was this a call from Chicago? I picked up the receiver, and the first thing I heard was a sound with which I would soon become very familiar. It was the whir and buzzing of a very long distance connection. It took longer than usual for me to hear a voice, and the words were somewhat broken. And then it hit me! This wasn't from Illinois—it was an overseas call! A very overseas call! I wasn't prepared.

"Marsh, is that you?" Even over 12,000 miles I could hear the concern in Ron's voice. "Marsh?"

I tried to sound composed. "Ron. How are you? What's wrong? Why are you calling me?"

He said he couldn't wait to call because he missed us all so much. He had called home and the sitter had given him this number. He wasn't happy. He wanted to know what was going on. Of course he did. (I still felt then that my visit to California was only a temporary thing. I didn't want him to know the truth.) I told him all the mental strain of the past few months had gotten to me and I had come to California to visit my friend Susan (who had been in our wedding) and to have some peace and quiet for a couple of days to regain my strength emotionally and physically. Ron liked Susan. I thought he believed my story. I think he wanted to believe it.

"Are you still coming over here with me?" he asked. It was a hint that perhaps he anticipated the worst.

"Of course I am, Silly," I replied. I believed it then.

It was after this call that the battle began to rage like a fire within me. It was a spiritual battle between the forces of the enemy and the Kingdom of God. I belonged to the Kingdom. What was happening to me? What was I to do about it? The need returned to be with my children and to have them close to me. Confusion and conviction at the same time. I was being pulled from two very strong directions, and you can be sure the devil had no intention of losing this one. His laughter was ringing in my ears, and I was walking around in some sort of spiritual daze wondering, "I wonder what that noise is"!

I called Craig at work and told him it was time for me to go home. I had plans to attend to before leaving the country with the children. He came to meet me right away. A sadness came over him that I have never seen in a man. He didn't plead with me then or try to stop me. That would have only served to make me smug. The means the enemy used to dig deeper into my being was this very genuine depression and sadness that made me feel sorry for Craig. He was quiet when he drove me to the airport and waited with me for my plane. He held me tightly and looked at me longingly and desperately. Tears came to him as I boarded the plane—no words but the ones that could effect me the most: "I love you".

Upon arrival back in Chicago I still faced a thirty minute drive home. The blinding tears, the perspiration, the confusion and the determination were things I would soon be living with constantly.

I thanked my friend when I arrived home, paid her and breathed a sigh of relief when she left me alone with my children. I took them in my arms and found comfort in their presence. The house was a mess but very still. Lyndsay and Joshua were so glad to have me home. All I wanted was to be with them and have the rest of the world just go away. I felt so lost in my sin that I couldn't face God to ask for help. I knew I was in the wrong, but I just knew I could fix it—then I would seek God again. I had to fix it.

The three of us were together for barely a half hour when the phone rang. "Get your composure, Marsha," I told myself. "Hurry up, Mrs. Wonderful, you can put your mask back on now and no one will know."

It was Ron. I knew he was weeping or had been. He announced, "I have just one thing to ask you and I want the truth. Were you with another man in San Francisco?"

It broke me completely. How did he know? In that brief moment I saw no reason to lie any more. But I was so lost and my ability to reason so diminished that I could utter only a barely distinguishable "yes".

Silence.

A click on the line told me I had another call coming in. I asked Ron to let me get rid of the call and I would be back. "Hold on," I muttered through my own tears.

It was Craig. Over and over again he pleaded. "Marsha, come back to me. I'll do anything. Honey, come back. Marsha, I'll marry you, I will. Please come back to me."

Fear engulfed me. Reason left me. Guilt pulled on me. Longing tugged at me.

> *"The Lord sees everything you do, and he watches where you go. An evil man will be caught in his wicked ways; the ropes of his sins will tie him up. He will die because he does not control himself, and he will be held captive by his foolishness."*
> Proverbs 5:21-23

I was sinking.

Eyes closed, I quietly hung up and feebly attempted to put my household in order. I couldn't bring myself to talk with anyone.

Chapter 5

THE PATTERN TAKES HOLD

The next week of my life went by more slowly than any I could remember. The only physical function I was able to perform was to care for my children. Even small children sense a mother's tensions and anxieties. I wanted them to be kept from feeling the pain of this difficult time and what it was doing to me. My efforts didn't work very well.

Ron called again and ordered me to see a lawyer and obtain an immediate divorce. Then he would call and try to talk us both out of it. Again and again he would call, not knowing what to do. For me, it was as though I had known all along it would come to this. I attempted to justify what I was doing and had done by convincing myself that Ron had never been what he should have been and shouldn't be surprised that I would turn to someone else to satisfy the needs he did not fulfill.

He did not fulfill! I blamed Ron for not meeting my needs and giving me a reason for going against all my principles. I blamed someone else! It was the only way I could keep from acknowledging that I was the one at fault. Many times I had heard the wonderful words of Jesus from scripture which remind us:

> *"I am the vine and you are the branches. If any remain
> in me and I remain in them, they produce much fruit.
> But without me they can do nothing."*
> John 15:5

I had never held God's hand tightly enough and now loosened the hold too greatly and looked in wrong places for fulfillment.

Our new spiritual nature, a gift at the time our lives are given to Christ in commitment, is in constant battle with our unrenewed mind which was trained by the nature we were born with and is bent on having its own way. Each of us have weak points that perhaps we think no one knows about but us. We forget that Satan knows and preys upon that very thing. We are admonished in I Peter 2:11 to

> *". . .avoid the evil things your bodies want to do that
> fight against your soul."*

God is well aware of what that war, that spiritual battle, can do to a Christian, and if that one who belongs to Christ allows Satan the victory, the price is ALWAYS too high. It was at this point that the Lord went into battle for me.

> *". . .we have the Lord our God to help us and
> to fight our battles."*
> II Chronicles 32:8

I am His child. I was His child then. I will always be His child. He knew what lay ahead if I did not turn from this worthless pursuit. I'm sure He was fully aware of the cost of this temporal euphoria. As I can clearly see now, God made a bend in the road to provide a way out before it was too late.

> *"The only temptation that has come to you is that which*
> *everyone has. But you can trust God, who will not*
> *permit you to be tempted more than you can stand. But*
> *when you are tempted, he will also give you*
> *a way to escape so that you will*
> *be able to stand it."*
> I Corinthians 10:13

But I didn't want to escape, and I didn't consider this a worthless pursuit. I saw it as a dream come true. To me there was nothing temporal about my relationship with Craig any longer. I was sure I could change anything about him that posed a problem. For some reason I was convinced that I could be a witness to him at the same time I was in direct disobedience to the Word of God in the pursuit of adultery. "God will see," I thought. "It would work out perfectly!" Instead, however, I am sure Jesus wept for me.

My behavior became very inconsistent and erratic. Close friends were well aware that Ron was far away and I was alone but still living in our house. I had totally withdrawn from any public or social life. I was told that I sounded nervous and looked exhausted all the time when a friend would try to visit or see if I had any needs. I was curt to the point of rudeness if someone would call. I covered my tracks and either denied my behavior or made up lies to hide what I was doing and thinking. But my Christian friends, particularly my closest one, would not leave me then. Though no one at that time knew what was happening, so many sensed my hurt and began talking about my strange behavior. One friend called to say she couldn't believe what she had heard about me and began to cry as she blurted out: "You have deceived us all!" I will never forget that.

What's worse, the concern of my friends did not at any point deter me. My mind was made up. Even their love did not stop me. It was God reaching out to me, it was His love coming through them, but my answer was 'no'.

A couple who were special to us called me from Southern California one day in the midst of my turmoil. Annie said she felt a need to call and shared that she and Bob had a very uneasy feeling about me for several days. Though we had written often, we rarely called one another long distance. I was surprised, but looking back I can see that God was continuing to reach out to me. When I heard her voice I couldn't bear the lies any more. Besides, Annie and Bob were far away. They could not interfere, and they would learn the truth sooner or later. I preferred that they learn it from me. All I remember of that call was Annie's gentle pleadings between her quiet sobs: "Oh, Marsha, no, no." She and Bob, a Christian psychologist, loved Ron and me. For several weeks they spent a great deal of money on long distance calls trying to help me see the reality of what I was doing. I loved them enough to listen but not enough to stop.

Satan knew by now that he had to fight to keep me in darkness before God's attempts to save me from this destruction succeeded. It wasn't ten days after I left California that Craig called from Chicago O'Hare airport and announced his arrival! I am sure my reaction was very predictable by the enemy, and he was right. As soon as I heard Craig's voice, a sense of comfort came over me. I could leave behind all the pleading and preaching and loneliness. All I wanted was Craig's arms around me and his assurance that everything would be alright. Today I can scarcely believe I chose his comfort rather than God's. How I could have been that totally deceived goes beyond my understanding. I was not aware of how deeply I was grieving my Savior nor how jealous He had become that I had allowed a mere man I barely knew to take His place in my heart and life and throw away all His blessings. It is something I will personally never comprehend. But God was not going to quit yet. I was the only quitter in this circumstance.

When I met Craig off and on those three days, I became mesmerized by him. He was full of promises. He believed there was no hope for my marriage, and why shouldn't he? I certainly wasn't honoring it. He began to concentrate on us and his plans for us—wild, wonderful plans for what we would do and have together. He filled my mind with what his wealth and prestige could give me just by the way he flaunted it. His attentions of me were constant and intense. We began to plan a future between us one step at a time. I ignored how the word 'marriage' made him flinch ever so slightly.

There were two very distinct patterns of thought emerging within me that would be used to hasten, secure and ensure my ultimate destruction. The deeper I allowed myself to fall into this web of superficial luxury, the more I became cradled in the arms of deception. So gullible was I that my attitude completely changed in a matter of weeks from a growing and vibrant Christian to a woman filled with fear. What kind of fear? Well, it was more of a desperation born of fear. I became so desperate in my thinking of how far I had strayed from God that I felt defeated, ashamed. I had taken things too far. There was no turning back now. How sad. Secondly, because of that hopelessness caused by shame and guilt, I began to put all my hope in Craig instead, desperate to make it work so I wouldn't wind up with nothing and no one.

As incredible as this all may sound, it wasn't the worst part. I believed I was completely rational!

Chapter 6

BLINDED EYES – DEADENED HEART

My decision had been officially made. Once I quietly broke fellowship with friends and believers, I began to carry out my plans. God continued to lovingly attempt to gain my attention in many ways and through many people. It is true that He never leaves us. If He seems far away, it's only because we have done the shifting.

I made arrangements by phone with Ron for the division of our property and storage of his belongings while he was overseas. I packed my things and took Lyndsay and Joshua to my parents' home in New Mexico, which would soon become like a retreat to me.

My parents were devastated. They both loved Ron and totally disagreed with what I was doing but never stopped loving me. They fought the temptation to become involved, and were torn between being supportive of me and washing their hands of me. My father urged Ron to return to the U.S. immediately, but I supposed doing so would only jeopardize his job, and I'm not sure he felt he could do anything anyway. Many times my parents discussed the situation with me but ultimately gave up at my determination and independent attitude. They did everything they could to help me through this time in my life, especially in caring for and protecting the children from experiencing the strain of it. In their love they gave unselfishly of themselves, their resources and their time to help heal the hurt we were all suffering. When I finally realized the toll it was taking on their lives, I quit commuting to San Francisco from New Mexico. Instead, I moved out there to be near Craig. Everything that had once been important to me, except for my children, was no more. Now all I had was Craig, and he was clinging to me as selfishly and desperately as I was clinging to him. He was worth everything to me.

God's love for me moved continually in each new circumstance as the weeks and months went by. He spoke to me very clearly through close Christian friends, and His words always beckoned, announcing peace. Annie and Bob, for instance, never gave up as they ministered to me with the greatest love I have ever known before or since from friends in the Body of Christ. Unselfishly they prayed and with great faith they did everything they could and were shown of God to help me avoid hurting myself and those I loved. Yes, there were times when I stepped back and tried to look at what I was doing. I did turn to them from time to time in my last vain attempts to heed God's calling. I hadn't forgotten my place in the Kingdom. It was the reason I experienced such tremendous conviction while I pursued my misdirected desires. I was being pulled so hard in two directions, and there were times, too, when I began to question myself and whether I could remain sane through this struggle. Still, I was the perpetrator of my own circumstance—not Ron, not Craig, and certainly not God. I was allowing this struggle in my life when I could have resisted it.

Soon the awareness that I was disobedient and dishonest with God became more and more apparent to me. It saddens me to know that I did not love Him enough to trust Him.

Interestingly, though, I did not see myself so much in sin at the time as simply 'in love'. In my mind I was too much 'in love' to give it all up. Prayer was hard for me because of shame, and turning to Craig was easy because when I was with him I didn't have to look at the wicked or injurious side of what I was doing. Because Craig did not know God in any sense of the word and would not listen when I did try to share God's love with him, he just worked to convince me that as long as we 'loved' each other we couldn't be wrong in what we were doing. Two grown people so deceived.

The truth was that it wasn't love I had for Craig; I wasn't 'in love' with him. I was 'in lust' with him. I had an addiction to him that was as permeating as any other kind of destructive addiction. I couldn't break the addiction because I didn't want to. For some reason I had to have him and believed in and trusted his promises above anyone's. My self-esteem quickly disappeared. If I didn't manage to hold on to Craig now, I saw myself left with nothing and no one, and that fearful vision began haunting me.

At this time it became more and more important to face some hard choices about the future. . .pretty hard to do when you can't even get a sane grip on the present! Ron and I spent hours and hundreds of dollars negotiating our settlement by phone over the 12,000 miles between us. I assured him of my care of Lyndsay and Joshua. I loved them so much and never, ever stopped caring for their needs, particularly that of clamoring to shield them in this crisis. Much as I loved them, my blinded eyes, my guilt and shame had me convinced of my worthlessness as a mother as well as a wife. I began to believe the lie that I had worth only in Craig's eyes and that there was no turning back. Selfishness and Craig reigned supreme in my heart, and fear was Chairman of the Board!

> *"Being afraid of people can get you into trouble, but if you trust the Lord, you will be safe."*
> Proverbs 29:25

In the midst of this inner turmoil I was forced to make many decisions that were to affect the future of everyone in my life. As I can plainly see now, I was in no emotional state whatsoever to make critical judgments and determinations then—not the kind with life-long ramifications. I was no longer walking with God, so I was completely blinded to all Truth. My fragile state of mind did not allow me to foresee any consequences; I could only try to do my best under the circumstances. Think about this: what kind of 'best' could come from such a strained and confused spirit, such a bound and fearful heart? I'll tell you what kind of 'best' it was.

It was Satan's best.

> *"He has blinded their eyes, and he has closed their minds. Otherwise they would see with their eyes and understand in their minds and come back to me and be healed."*
> John 12:40

By my opening the door, the enemy worked to prevent any normal future with my children in this madness. Only a blinded spirit could have acted with such foolishness and lack of reason.

Craig had already planned for his future and made sure I understood that his plan would not change. He owned a breathtakingly beautiful 50-foot Grand Banks yacht he had named 'Mistress'. It was by far the most important part of his life. He told me once that I was the only person or thing in his life he had ever allowed to take precedence over

Mistress. As a matter of fact, his friends were baffled that he even claimed there was someone who meant more to him than Mistress did. Sadly, I counted on that. Incredibly, I believed it. I bought it all—hook, line and sinker. I basked in it, relished it, practically wore it around my neck like a medal! Craig told me again and again that he and Mistress would be taking a world cruise soon. He would retire and live on his grand and wonderful yacht. Of course if we were to marry, I would be living on it, too, or so he said. Well, that's got to make a girl plan to fit into the scheme of things if she wants her man, right? And you can bet I wanted that man. Naturally, I made plans accordingly. There was one problem: Lyndsay and Joshua. They would have school soon and I wanted them to have as normal a life as possible. I saw only misery for them if they were to live with 'us'—private schools, full-time nannies and no family life. It all loomed so big before me, so f-o-r-e-v-e-r.

I didn't want to do that to my children, but I was not going to say no to Craig, either. After all, I had been taught that a woman's husband should come first.

My next decision, then, was based entirely on intuition and a genuine attempt to do the best for Lyndsay and Joshua under the circumstances. I agreed with Ron on joint custody of our children. I would determine (after he returned permanently to the United States) whether or not he could provide the kind of environment the children needed. As long as communication was never hindered, he would have physical custody of our babies during the school year and I would have them summers and holidays. I had to make a choice and that is the one I made and why I made it. Did I think for one moment that things might change? No. I just signed my name, and in so doing signed away my children.

Chapter 7

SINKING FAST

In February Ron made his first trip back to the U.S. Our divorce hearing was scheduled in Chicago. I gave Ron time to take the children back to be with his family in Wisconsin before the hearing. I remember thinking how tan and slim he looked. The Saudi Arabian sun had been good for him. I realized later that he had lost a great deal of weight only under the burden and duress of the loss of his family and his inability to eat and sleep well.

Ron had come back to the States with a hopeful heart. He wanted to believe I would not go through with my plans. He felt maybe his return would change my mind, and he was wild to see his children again. I didn't know where he stood spiritually; he never shared that.

I checked into my hotel the night before the hearing. Craig called to make sure I was still committed only to him. Pressure from all sides. But there was a difference this time.

I was back where I had started. . .back home in Lake County where my friends were. I began to feel claustrophobic just being there, aware of the totality of what I was doing. I even wanted to hide my face as I walked into the hotel lobby. The bondage I felt was suffocating. I glanced down at the walnut-sized diamond ring Craig had given me and found comfort there. I would put it away if I was to be around anyone I knew, especially Ron.

Then there was Sharon, my best friend. I hadn't even told her where I was going when I left, only that it was for someone else, that my marriage was over. I remembered how she had stared at me in disbelief but hugged me, wished me well, and said she would pray for me continually. I had to call her. I wanted to hear her tell me I was still acceptable. How could I think that I would be? When I talked with her, Sharon said she still cared about me as much as ever but could not condone my behavior. In our conversation God did a spectacular thing! He was going to speak to me again—firmly. Sharon put a prayer chain together.

Within an hour and until after midnight I received several calls at the hotel from friend after friend who had been in prayer for me when the whispers started to fly. Not knowing exactly what had happened to me, they prayed to hear from me and to be of help if at all possible. That's the love of God, dear friends! That is the Hound of Heaven moving in lives. Every woman who called me that night truly begged me to reconsider what I was doing to myself and all who loved me. One special lady I remember told me, "Marsha, you think you have pain now? It's nothing compared to what you'll know if you go through with this."

I cried all night. My body trembled and I perspired until I was saturated with the sweat of a guilty and worried mind. Unfortunately, I was so lost in sin that I couldn't see the truth plainly in front of me. Instead of repenting and running to the arms of my husband, I shrank back in guilt and shame. Satan told me I was unworthy of those people and my husband any more, and I believed it. I believed it was too late to turn back! I bought a terrible deception that I had gone too far and could never be whole again or face my friends or Ron or his family again. I had only begun to pay the price.

For these reasons I kept my appointment with the judge

early the next morning. I don't remember much about the hearing. I draw almost a complete blank at the thought of it. Ron stayed with the children and did not attend the hearing with his attorney.

It only took ten minutes. Just ten minutes of numbness and the judge slammed the gavel on his massive desk and declared my marriage dead. I staggered out of that courtroom with my unfeeling attorney and had to be helped to the elevator because I was very faint. I began to sob. Not so coincidently, the person who came to my aid was Ron's attorney, a Jewish man. There in the hallway of that court-house where man degrades man, I wept in his arms.

When I returned to the hotel, there was Ron in the lobby with the children, trying hard to hold back his own tears. I had never seen him look at me the way he did then and I was never to see it again. He simply said, "I didn't think you'd really go through with it."

The children and I caught an immediate flight back to San Francisco. Flying had never bothered me. This time I threw up all the way back while the children mercifully slept.

> *"Whoever is stubborn after being corrected many times*
> *will suddenly be hurt beyond cure."*
> Proverbs 29:1

Chapter 8

FOR NOW I'll JUST DO THIS

The next twelve weeks would be monumental in the pattern of events stemming from the dissolution of my marriage to Ron. So much was about to occur that would forever mar my life with scars. What I didn't see then was the extent to which God was going to take His love for me and how greatly He was about to work in this bottomless pit into which I was tumbling deeper by the day. Never for a moment did He abandon my situation. I can only share His power and love with hindsight because my eyes were so blinded all the way through the fire! I couldn't see because I wouldn't see.

"When you pass through the waters, I will be with you."
Isaiah 43:2

Upon our arrival back in San Francisco, the children and I were greeted with two dozen of the most beautiful roses I'd ever seen. Craig appeared fearful of something (just enough for me to notice). Could he have worried that I wouldn't return?

I remained emotionally and physically sick over the events of the previous few days, but I hid it from Craig. It was so hard then to express myself in any way either to him or to the children. I tried to smile and I wanted to function normally, thinking the anguish and disgust that was breaking my spirit would leave me. Besides, I kept telling myself I was back with Craig and didn't have to face anybody or anything contrary to my 'happiness' as I saw it—at least not in the foreseeable future. But the harder I tried to put away the thoughts, the more they plagued my mind. Over and over again it all taunted me until I awoke in a cold sweat late the next night compelled to do something about it. There was a battle going on inside me that drew me through the darkness to the telephone. I knocked over the vase of roses as I switched on a light to dial the number I knew so well. It had been thirty-six hours since Ron and I had parted in Chicago, and it was mid-afternoon in Saudi Arabia.

I dialed without thinking about it first. I didn't even know if it would be answered at the other end yet. I just did it and then, miraculously, the familiar deep voice was faint but unmistakable in reply:

"Hello? Hello?" I swallowed hard, but no words would come to me, only a river of tears. "Hello?" he said again.

"Ron?"

"Yes. Marsh, is that you?"

"Yes. Will you talk to me for a minute?"

He was amazed. He had just then walked in his house after arriving in Arabia from his overseas flight. In fact, he said, he'd been in the door only fifteen minutes.

"Ron, I can't live with this! I can't go on like this. I have no peace. I just know God is trying to say something to me. I've been sick for two days. Help me. Tell me I can come home. Tell me you'll forgive me. What can I do? Are you still my friend?"

Twelve thousand miles between us again and nothing legal binding us anymore. It was the middle of the night for me and the end of a gut-wrenching, thirty-hour transcontinental trip for him. Would he reply or would he hang up on me?

"All right, listen to me," he said with authority. "Do exactly what I tell you. Call Annie and Bob and ask if you can stay with them. Don't think about anything. . .just pack your things, load the car and get down to Los Angeles first thing in the morning. Wait there to hear from me. The company doesn't know we're divorced. I'll start the processing to get you over here. Just get out of that place as fast as you can and go where you and the kids will be safe until I can get you on a plane to Jeddah. Did you hear me?"

"Yes, oh my god, yes! But what if Annie and Bob won't take us in?"

"Just call them. It'll be all right. Trust me."

No one can imagine the haste and determination that made me forge ahead those next few hours. I didn't even think about what I was doing. I packed through the rest of the night. It's a wonder I didn't get mugged while I was carrying things to and from the car in the darkness of those early morning hours. When dawn came and the children woke, I gave them both a hug and asked them to help me get ready for a very fun trip. We made a game of it, and there were no hindrances.

I was leaving a note for my manager and a note for Craig when I remembered the stunning, brilliant diamond on the third finger of my left hand. I stared at it for what I thought was one last time, then decided where I would leave it with the good-bye note. In my note I said nothing truthful because I secretly wanted to know I still had a hold on Craig even though I was planning never to see him again. I did not mention that I was compelled to do this because it was what God wanted of me, to live up to my Christian commitment by taking a stand for what was right. Perhaps the reason for that was because I wanted to try to have the best of both worlds. I wanted to be obedient to God, but I didn't realize the hardness of my heart as I still did not want to let go of Craig completely. I forgot what God says in Matthew 6:24:

> *"No one can serve two masters. The person will hate one master and love the other, or will follow one master and refuse to follow the other. You cannot serve both God and worldly riches."*

I would deal with my wavering thoughts and feelings later. For now I'll just do this and maybe things will get better.

I was only after relief. I was not after God's will. My mistake here was in not reaching out to God as He was reaching out to me. He was talking to me and working in my life as plainly as if He had paid me a personal visit. I only saw a way out of a turmoil—or at least a possibility for a change that might lead to a way out. I immediately began to manipulate the situation and attempt to accomplish things and events in my own understanding. I never prayed. I never thanked my wonderful Lord. I never asked for His guidance; I simply tried to consider myself obedient. I knew it was scriptural that I return to my husband, but I neglected to give God control. I still held the reigns. I guess my thinking at the time was to go along with what was right as long as it satisfied all my own selfish desires.

> *"Trust the Lord with all your heart, and don't depend on your own understanding. Remember the Lord in all you do, and He will give you success."*
> Proverbs 3:5,6
>
> *"These people show honor to me with words, but their hearts are far from me."*
> Matthew 15:8

Annie and Bob could not have been happier. They saw a way to help a broken relationship that was important to them and opened their home with great love and expectation. When the children and I arrived there later that day, we all hugged each other anxiously. I told Annie and Bob the last thing I saw as I left the Bay Area had been Craig's champagne-colored Mercedes pulling up the driveway as I was pulling away.

Then came the waiting, and it was misery. I was so impatient. Annie and Bob were more than generous and a great example for me in all we were going through. Lyndsay, Joshua and I used that time to spend many happy hours alone together, too. While we waited for Ron's company to phone and say we were set to go, we busily filled our days with visits to Disneyland, Knotts Berry Farm and Marineland. I loved those days. My babies and I shared so many quality moments together that warm my heart when I reflect on them. Annie and Bob and I just loved those children right through those days.

Annie and Bob both worked. While they were away during the week I would entertain the children and keep house for Annie. But it soon became difficult for the five of us to live in that tiny two-bedroom apartment, and the anticipation of my trip was quickly driving me to distraction. Satan used these conflicts as a new avenue of attack, and I became very weak in the flesh. I could pray as long as Annie and Bob were there to lean on, but when they weren't, I was alone with my thoughts and longings.

It was just at that time that Craig found me. He had flown to Southern California, and with the number he had obtained, phoned me to plead with me to see him one more time.

The battle resumed with more force than I had known before. God's spirit within me told me no! Craig told me yes.

This grown man began pleading with me in the same way he always had, the same old way to which I'd given in a million times before. Promises, promises! Visions of opulence, honey-dripping scenes of passionate moments and undying love were spoken to me again and again. Craig couldn't wait to show me the house he had just bought for 'us' in Hillsborough, one of the most elite suburbs in the country. Mistress was waiting to take us on a honeymoon cruise to Mexico, and his friends all missed me and wanted to see us back together again.

God was saying:

> *"Come to me, all of you who are tired and have heavy loads, and I will give you rest."*
> Matthew 11:28
>
> *"Be humble under God's powerful hand so he will lift you up when the right time comes."*
> I Peter 5:6,7

But Craig was <u>there</u>! He was there and I could see him. I didn't want to wait. My human nature wanted something tangible—and I was still controlling my own life. "Thank you, God, but no thanks. I guess I want this just too much."

The Lord is right. We cannot serve two masters. And the world says, "If it feels good, do it." Well, it felt good, very good, and I did it. I was persuaded again. While Annie and Bob were at work, it was easy to sneak away in my cowardice.

I packed my things again with Craig's help and went back to San Francisco with him.

Chapter 9

MY LONGING – GOD'S REACHING

I was going to remain in this turbulence of soul for a long time. No one knew but God and me how great the storm was that raged inside me. I wanted Craig so badly and believed him so strongly that no warnings kept me from him. At the same time, I spent many hours in solitude, hurting in a way I can't describe over my damaged relationship with my God. If I had just picked up my Bible, He could have spoken to me from the words of Solomon:

> *"It is so good when wishes come true, but fools hate to stop doing evil. Spend time with the wise and you will become wise, but the friends of fools will suffer. Trouble always comes to sinners, but good people enjoy success."*
> Proverbs 13:19-21

Why didn't I choose one way of life or the other?

> *"I know what you do, that you are not hot or cold.*
> *I wish that you were hot or cold! But because you are*
> *lukewarm — neither hot, nor cold — I am ready to spit*
> *you out of my mouth. You say, 'I am rich, and I have*
> *become wealthy and do not need anything.' But you do*
> *not know that you are really miserable, pitiful, poor,*
> *blind, and naked. I advise you to buy from me gold*
> *made pure in fire so you can be truly rich. Buy from me*
> *white clothes so you can be clothed and so you can*
> *cover your shameful nakedness. Buy from me medicine*
> *to put on your eyes so you can truly see. I correct and*
> *punish those whom I love. So be eager to do right,*
> *and change your hearts and lives."*
> Revelation 3:15-19

The truth is that I had made a choice. The fact that my emotions swung back and forth was a choice. God says there is a vast difference. A repentant heart turns from the sin and never looks back or goes back.

Did I think, for even a minute, that maybe Craig wasn't worth it if he rejected God now? No. And if he rejected that love and forgiveness now, what made me so sure he would ever accept it? Because I was going to solve all my own problems, thank you very much. Craig would come to the love of God just because of me! So sad. The contradictions in my life had devoured too much of it. I never once gave credence to the fact that Craig could never believe me later if I was abusing my position before God so greatly now and dishonoring all I said I believed in! I would only become a stumbling block to him, and I was a fool to think Satan's plan for me was to prosper!

> "...When the floods came, the house quickly fell and
> was completely destroyed."
> Luke 6:49b

By this time, I was an emotional basket case and a physical wreck. When Craig and I weren't together, I would either waste away in confusion or fight to put it out of my mind and concentrate on the children, a project or ANYTHING! With Craig, I put on my mask and pretended nothing was wrong. I couldn't explain this lack of peace, and I didn't want to be asked to try. Instead, I covered up my hurt, which only intensified the pain. What a terrible, vicious and deadly cycle! Now I lived with the belief that since I had made my bed, I had to lie in it.

I hadn't heard from Ron but imagined how he felt. His letters to the children had stopped. There was a long silence between us that I pretended to ignore. I wished for a chance to explain and then was glad I didn't have to. I would push away the thought of Ron so far away, so lonesome for his kids and his life torn apart by what I'd done. Guilt pressured me more than ever. Shame added its waste until my self-worth gave up and went down in defeat.

God was not finished with me yet. In mid-April I received a phone call late one morning. The children were playing at the home of a friend and I was alone. As I picked up the receiver I heard the unmistakable buzz of overseas long distance and took a deep breath as I realized it was Ron.

There was only one reason for the call and he got right to the point. I could tell he was trying hard to gain and keep some composure. "Marsha," he began, "God has told me to call you one more time." It was the only time I had ever heard him mention God's name. "Marsha, I love you. Please don't marry that guy. Come here with me where you belong."

At that moment everything stopped for me—the world

quit turning. It was as if I stepped away from my body, turned around and watched in anticipation. I couldn't believe what I heard. This time he was asking me! What next? What more could happen to confuse me? I didn't want to make choices any longer. I was afraid of myself—afraid any choices I made would be wrong. But one word Ron said made the difference; the word that made up my mind for me: God.

Incredibly, I dropped everything again, grabbed the children and headed back to Annie and Bob's. No note this time. The last thing I did was tear up the pre-nuptial agreement from Craig's attorney that arrived in the mail the same day—the one he forgot to tell me about.

Without realizing it, I was living through the greatest display of real love I've ever witnessed. Annie and Bob never quit believing in me then. They never rejected me—only my behavior, which they saw as injurious to me. They loved me right past my lies and deception and saw me completely through the eyes of a loving God. I can't count the number of times they told me how God had instructed them in prayer to remain patient and faithful to our friendship. They never worried about the inconvenience—to them there never was any. I'll always remember Annie's consistent, sincere smile and gentle spirit and Bob's loving attitude and strong grip on to the principles I had discarded. They operated entirely in God's method of love and forgiveness. They were so attuned to His leading that I believe they were aware of what Satan had in mind for my life and tried to help me avoid it.

Yes, they took us in again. I remember well the birthday parties we had for Lyndsay and Joshua, whose special days are only five days apart. I can picture still the trips to church together and to our favorite restaurant afterwards for those terrific teriyaki burgers and homemade pie. When I close my eyes I can still feel the sensation of peace, warmth and acceptance on the evenings we spent sharing old times together and looking hopefully to the future as Lyndsay and

Joshua would fall asleep in someone's arms. And there were the moments they would cry with me in a church service when I heard God speaking and break down in sorrow over what we were all going through. We prayed for deliverance from the addiction still raging inside me, still holding me.

Twice I gave in to Craig's insistence and met with him to talk about our dilemma. I really planned to leave the country this time, but my 'love' for him caused me to want to avoid hurting him; I wanted to be gentle when breaking off our relationship. Here again, the enemy worked to blind me. While I attempted to let him down easily and with an attitude of kindness, I was again deceiving Annie and Bob by seeing him secretly. Here I was, convinced that my example of courtesy would help Craig see what God was doing in my life, but he only saw that he got to me every time he tried. I told him God needed my willing heart to repair my broken marriage, but Craig saw my willing heart as his and his alone. I should have truly repented and gone on with my life, but my subconscious would not let go of the need to keep some kind of hold on that man. Pride and arrogance became involved. The Bible says:

> *"Pride will destroy a person;*
> *a proud attitude leads to ruin."*
> **Proverbs 16:18**

Chapter 10

WHERE YOUR TREASURE IS

It was a balmy California evening in late spring when we left the United States. Annie and Bob made the trek with Lyndsay, Joshua and me to Los Angeles International for our final good-byes. I stared out the window of the terminal at the huge L-1011 that was about to take me to my destiny in a land far away. "What waits for me?" I whispered. I was trembling just enough to notice.

"Mommie, come on!" Lyndsay brought me back to reality. "Will we see Daddy soon?" Oh. . .the innocence and tenderness of children. . .the impact we have on that innocence can be as damaging as it is subtle.

"Soon, Princess, soon. He's waiting anxiously for you." Such a beautiful child, with a sensitivity not unlike her mother's. Sometimes I am caught gazing into her lovely face and pulling her close with no explanation. Then she will demand one. "Oh, Honey, I just love you so, so much," I tell her proudly. Joshua had fallen asleep on Annie's lap.

Then our flight was called! I handed my car keys to Bob for safekeeping until our return, silently embraced him and Annie good-bye, took the hands of my children and walked toward my future without looking back. An ominous and dreadful feeling came over me as I watched the lights of Los Angeles and the security of my country disappear into the horizon.

My spirit was wounded and still in great turmoil. Late into the night I gaped in wonder at the endless chasm of sea below me and tried to forget that I would never see Craig again when I had come so close to having him. I was frightened of Ron and couldn't see how God could possible restore our respect for one another. I guess I was seeing God through the eyes of human limitation rather than obedient faith. It looked impossible to me, but I had to try. Prayer eluded me because my spiritual support was gone. Annie and Bob weren't with me now. Something told me, "You're on your own, Girl!" I knew better—I KNEW BETTER—but my fears and anxieties clutched and paralyzed me.

> *"Everything I feared and dreaded has happened to me. I have no peace or quietness. I have no rest, only trouble."*
> Job 3:25-26

I thought we'd never get to Amsterdam. The children slept through the night, but peace eluded me hour after hour. I allowed myself to be taunted with visions of the 'good life' I left behind and began to tell myself I was a fool to think the threadbare relationship between my former husband and myself could really be repaired. God didn't look big enough to me then to get the job done, and I knew I wasn't.

> *". . .store your treasures in heaven where they cannot be destroyed by moths or rust and where thieves cannot break in and steal them.*
> *Your heart will be where your treasure is."*
> Matthew 6:19-21

I was not going to admit to myself or anyone else that my heart was still in San Francisco with Craig, his possessions and his promises. I wanted to believe, and I wanted others to believe, that I was going to Arabia in obedience to God. But my treasure then lay behind me about 8,000 miles in San Francisco and with it my heart. You cannot serve two masters.

I never thought of the desire I had for Craig as an addiction. Not until after the fact. An addiction is a devotion to a practice or habit or to something habit-forming to such an extent that cessation causes severe trauma.

It is absolutely no wonder then, since my addiction, my treasure, was what I saw in Craig, that my true heartfelt desire in this situation was not toward the Lord. Jesus says:

> *"The eye is a light for the body. If your eyes are good, your whole body will be full of light. But if your eyes are evil, your whole body will be full of darkness. And if the only light you have is really darkness, then you have the worst darkness."*
> Matthew 6:22-23

Something else I've learned through this experience is that we cannot turn from sin until we acknowledge that we are living in it. How would God get through my blindness? Would I ever see the truth?

We touched down in Amsterdam, Holland, about noon the following day. The teeming pace of this bustling city and its wonderful friendly people temporarily took my mind off my problem as the children and I carefully managed our way through Customs and out into the mainstream of life. I suddenly felt filled to the brim with a latent sense of excitement about where I found myself. The windmills, the tulips, the channel—it was all I had heard and read about and dreamed of. What a privilege to see it all.

A kind man directed us in broken English to a city bus which would take us to the hotel listed in our itinerary. He carried and loaded our bags, helped us on the bus, tipped his hat in farewell and plainly said "God bless you" as we parted. I've never forgotten.

The next flight to Jeddah, Saudi Arabia, would not leave until late the next morning. The three of us had jet lag right down to our toes and eagerly sought a restaurant for a quiet meal. Then we looked forward to a hot bath and a much-needed rest. At the suggestion of a family we met at the hotel, I took the children to a world-famous tulip garden on the outskirts of the city two hours before preparing for our flight the next day. The children were young and their attention span short, so the novelty wore off quickly. But I walked through the garden quietly with them, enjoying the magnificent display before me. The meticulously tended grounds as far as I could see in either direction were filled with an endless array of masterfully sculpt tulips in every conceivable color and shape. The beauty of it left me silent and took me far away from my circumstances for that brief moment in time. I was reminded again of the privilege that was mine.

There was a greater privilege afforded me, but I didn't see it as such. This trip was a miracle! God wanted to restore to me what sin in my life had all but destroyed. I didn't see the advantage, though, or the privilege—I only saw a duty, an obligation. But God still was not finished with me:

> *"This is what the Lord says: "The wise must not brag about their wisdom. The strong must not brag about their strength. The rich must not brag about their money. But if someone wants to brag, let him brag that*

> *I am the Lord, and that I am kind and fair, and that I do
> things that are right on earth. This kind of bragging
> pleases me," says the Lord."*
> Jeremiah 9:23-24

My pulse was racing when we boarded our plane for
Arabia. I knew I would be facing Ron soon and still didn't
know how to handle our reunion. I tried to pray "God, show
me how."

Late into the night, sleep still escaping me, I took a deep
breath as the lights of Jeddah appeared below. The
exhausting trip was almost over and a new adventure about
to begin. I touched up my hair and makeup in anticipation,
then quietly woke the children. My patience wore thin as
we deplaned and loaded with a multitude of Arabs into a
tiny bus for a trip to the terminal building. I wasn't sure I'd
find the children again!

The building drew closer by the moment. Before I
realized it we stopped at its door. I peaked through the
bodies surrounding me and I saw him. He was perched on a
railing just inside the door looking very conspicuous but
surprisingly indifferent. Ron was not given to much emotion.
Was he as unsure as I was about this whole thing?

I smiled broadly as we entered the terminal, but he didn't
notice. He quickly scooped up the children in his arms. They
were tired but very responsive to him. It wasn't until he put
Joshie up on his shoulders, took Lyndsay by her hand and
began to walk toward Customs that he looked at me and
acknowledged my presence. "Hi, Marsh."

I didn't blame Ron; he had every right to be leery of me,
but I was hurt. I tried to touch his arm, but he walked ahead
of me so quickly, I couldn't get close enough.

I stood aside somewhat and watched him with the children
as we waited to get through a long line at the Customs gate.

I glanced down at the Bible hidden in my carry-on luggage, disguised with a brown paper cover. I had had his name engraved on it. I wanted to drop it and run.

Chapter 11

TRYING, BUT FOR WHOM?

God's promises are unshakeable, and it is against His very nature to break a promise He has made to those who belong to Him.

> *"Be strong and brave. Don't be afraid of them and don't be frightened, because the Lord your God will go with you. He will not leave you or forget you."*
> Deuteronomy 31:6

Another certainty with which we live is the liberty of choice. Our freedom of will remains as effectual after a commitment to Christ as it is before. He encourages us to be strong and courageous because His wonderful promises can only come to pass as we yield to His will for our lives. It's guaranteed in writing! He reveals it in His Word, His love letter to us and in the Person of His Son, Jesus. God will not forget us, but we can easily forget Him. If we reflected more on the guarantees involved before we make the choice, we would probably more often make the right one. If we choose the path of the enemy, we have no certainties at all. The choice is ours.

Our first day in Saudi Arabia put me in a hazy cultural shock! I'm sure I walked around with my mouth open, gaping foolishly at all the strange phenomena around me. Jeddah is a teeming city where people are cautious, heat is suffocating, and where poverty and wealth, each to the extreme, live side by side. One moment you'd see costly modern skyscrapers designed with Western influence and catering heavily to Western tastes; the next moment you might be driving through a desolate neighborhood where dilapidated buildings house only a bed and clothesline on what is left of its roof. Expensive imported automobiles were parked in front of lavish shops where children begged in the doorways. Remains of demolished vehicles were everywhere on the roadside, left to rot in the Arabian sun following an accident. Shops catering only to the gold trade lined the streets looking like temples of Solomon. Next door to some were garbage heaps or fly-ridden vegetable stands. Men moved hastily around us wearing white toga-type garments with large white head coverings resembling wrapped beach towels. Women were draped in black, faces covered. The wealthy were decked in gold from their foreheads to their feet, yet still dressed in black and covered modestly. We drove two hundred miles north to the job site counting camels along the way and tiring quickly of the desert terrain which stretched as far as we could see.

The children were so good. Jet lag kept them asleep a great deal, which was probably best for them at the time. I was amazed at the luxurious conditions Ron pointed out when we arrived and drove through the various camps to our house. Ron had been assigned there only days before when his status had changed from single to family. He had done a nice job of decorating it comfortably for all of us. Everything was supplied: appliances, kitchenware, furniture, vacuum cleaner, linens—you name it. Included in a contractual employment agreement was free medical care and housing, much free entertainment, and a cost-of-living allowance over and above salary. It is difficult to entice people to work in this foreign land without offering substantial advantages.

I didn't feel well those first two or three days, so Ron took the children to the beach a few miles away. It was actually the coast of the Red Sea! If they weren't at the beach they were at one of several pools near the house where families met to bake in the hot Arabian sun.

We were nervous and touchy around each other, but I was very anxious to talk. Ron seemed to want to forget the discussions and get on with life. When he returned to work soon after our arrival, a tremendous sense of 'aloneness' settled in my spirit. I occupied time with the children and pressed my 'cope' button. It worked well, but I wondered how long it would last.

After four or five days, some friends of Ron's invited us to a dinner party in our honor as a welcoming gesture toward me. I was very touched. I tried to dress well and look my best because I sure wanted to make that good impression. Ron thought I was still making a stab at trying to be the center of attention. I guess I tried too hard.

The other Americans I met that night were good people who seemed sincere and well-meaning. Homemade wine was served; the sale of alcoholic beverages is strictly prohibited in Arabia, and it is imperative that all personnel honor the Muslim customs at all times. I didn't like the concoction, but I sipped on it to be polite. I made a point of mingling, something I've always been good at.

Around nine that evening I searched for Ron in the small crowd and spotted him laughing audibly across the room. No one has a better sense of humor or a better repertoire of jokes than Ron, and he had several buddies laughing with him in a far corner. I walked toward them but stopped in my tracks as I got close enough to see Ron clearly. His eyes were glassed over and his mannerisms getting showy, and I recognized the old signs that had always triggered fear in me. I smiled and walked the other way, determined to keep my distance and not make a scene. I didn't feel it was my place to say anything about his behavior—besides, I was scared to death of what reaction it might bring.

Women aren't allowed to drive in Arabia, so the short ride back to our house found me rigid with fear and totally quiet. I knew he knew that I knew! The babysitter lived close by, so Ron saw her home. When he returned, I was sitting nervously in the living room wondering how I was going to share the same bed with this man shaking with fear as much as I was. What happened next was a final blow for me.

"Don't get up," he shouted as he turned off the lights and lit a candle.

"Try not to wake the children," I asked him sternly.

"You just stay quiet and listen to me," he demanded, pointing a finger inches from my face. "I have some things to say to you that I've wanted to say for a long time, and you're going to listen and not move."

I said a silent prayer to let this be over soon. I recognized his need to get it all out—to voice some hurts he'd been bottling up for so long. I felt he was justified, but I was not prepared for the next forty-five minutes of verbal flogging I was about to endure. I was laughed at and cursed. I was called some of the filthiest names anyone has ever called me to my face. I heard stories of how his family really hated me and had questioned me all along. I was called a phoney, a liar and a hypocrite. My body, mind and spirit were insulted over and over again pointedly. I started to tremble, and my body shook itself into a cold sweat. I kept telling myself it was alright. He had a right to hate me and deserved a chance to lash out at me. I never opened my mouth but sat in silence in that dark room, making myself take what I knew I had coming. I was crying big, silent tears of loneliness and shame.

I didn't sleep all that night. The next day was just as I

expected—Ron had no idea what he had done, or so he claimed. I began to wonder what I was doing there and how I could ever tolerate living out my life this way.

In the three weeks that followed that awful night, two very strong forces were at work inside of me. Though I was enjoying what I was learning about living in this foreign country, I was daily becoming more and more hesitant around Ron. I tried to keep from admitting that I just didn't like him anymore. Time would heal it, I'd tell myself. We didn't take time to study the Word of God together and never opened the Bible study material I had successfully smuggled through Customs. I tried to look at it myself, but became defeated in my attempts because the enemy had me convinced that if we couldn't study together, what was the use? I threw myself into becoming Super Homemaker again just to become absorbed in SOMETHING. The children filled my days, and I began to look for ways to get involved in life at the compound by working cooperatively with other mothers. We lived from day to day with no more talk of our relationship, of God's involvement in it or where it was going. It became convenient to ignore the issue.

During this charade, the passing days would find me fatigued to the point of surprise in myself. Every day I noticed that I was more tired than the day before, no matter how much sleep I got at night. Within two weeks, I was falling onto the sofa every half hour or so as I became unable to move through the day without stopping constantly. Soon I quit taking the kids to the pool in the afternoons and lovingly asked them to play in their rooms or watch the VCR while Mommie got some rest. They would look to Daddy to entertain them when he got home. By the third week the fatigue had a companion: loss of appetite. I couldn't even go in to the kitchen or be around food because it nauseated me. It was a strain to prepare meals or get snacks for Lyndsay and Joshua. Ron began fixing his own lunches and preparing supper, too.

Fortunately, cooking was a pleasure for him. He had always liked it and didn't seem put out. The loss of appetite soon evolved into dry heaves, and I found myself involuntarily trying to empty my stomach when nothing was in it. We finally concluded that I was sick, but still contributed it to jet lag and stress. Then nights became totally sleepless and I spent them pacing the house hour after hour in quiet tears, trying not to waken anyone. What was wrong with me?

By our fourth week in Arabia, my misery caught up with me. Emotionally I was living nothing but a nightmare of play-acting, and physically I was deteriorating quicker each day and didn't know why. My birthday came, and for the first time in my life I had no joy over it. Just as he had done so successfully in my life in recent months, Satan used this vulnerable point in time to manifest himself again.

I was moving slowly around the house the morning of my birthday, trying to get some chores done. The phone rang. It was probably my parents calling across the miles to wish me a happy birthday. But it was Craig; he had found me again. Dear God. It was really him!

Craig mumbled something about finding the number on a phone bill and began verbally saturating me with pleading to forgive him if he had ever hurt me. I could ask anything I wanted and I could have it, but please, would I please come back to him? "Honey, I can't live without you," he said again and again. "I know I've been wrong about some things, but I'll change. All I want is you, I see that now. You're divorced from Ron; you don't have to stay there. Oh, Honey, say you'll come back. Do you need money? How much money do you need? I'll send anything. No, wait. I'll get my passport together and come and get you if I have to. He can't stop me! I'll find you. Marsha, please. I have your engagement ring in my hand. You haven't remarried him, I know you haven't. Sweetheart, please don't. I need you. It's your birthday, Marsh. Say you'll come back."

Dear God. Back to Square One. I couldn't believe all this! I couldn't believe it!

"Craig, it's true, I miss you. But I can't keep turning my life upside down. Don't you see what you're asking of me?" I was a mess.

That night at my birthday party I was only half there. Turmoil raged again, and it looked like the battle was going to Satan.

The phone calls kept coming and I weakened with each of them. His voice and promises were alluring compared with the struggle of my relationship with Ron. Pretty soon my conscience could keep the secret no longer. I had to tell Ron the truth. I had to do something, and I knew I wasn't hanging up the phone when the calls came.

This time his anger was unleashed. He looked at me in disgust and rage and said he'd rather be finally rid of me if that's the kind of woman I was. "Get out!" he demanded with unusual force. "Good riddance. Maybe we can all start living again if you just get the hell out of my life once and for all! He can have you! I'm finished with you! Just remember, when you walk out that door you're never coming back, do you understand that?"

I cried. He cried. We walked the house in silence again, both hearts breaking. This time Lyndsay and Joshua cried, too. This was a nightmare—it had to be! Things like this don't really happen in life—not to me—NOT TO ME! When would this nightmare end? I consoled myself with the fact that Ron had not laid a hand on me. I consoled myself with the false security that I could be with Craig again. If I could just get past this point and through the technicalities still facing me, I would make it. Back to Craig's arms. Back to his life, his promises, his acceptance. I would be alright. At least the decision was made. No more pulling from two directions. It had to end sometime. I just told myself I was making the right decision. I'd show them all—I really would!

We lived the next few days as if a great burden had been lifted from us. We were polite but distant. Once Ron commented that he felt like he was living with another man's wife. He whispered it without looking at me. I would rather have been stabbed in the heart, I think. What was I doing? In the name of heaven, what was I doing? Sadly, the last thing I did was turn to God. Shame now overcame me as if death warmed over. I tried to keep going from day to day as Ron began the arrangements to return me and the children to the States. But I wouldn't change my mind.

In an attempt to get through those awful days, I occasionally took the bus into town to shop with the children. When you're waiting, time goes by just too slowly. We had not yet told Lyndsay and Joshua of our plans. They were too young to understand. Besides, it would take weeks to complete the paperwork and get plane reservations to New York. Ron also had to explain all this to his company; he would have to cover up the real truth. I mulled it over in my mind constantly through those endless days and looked to my children for my comfort. When I did leave the house, I could never stay away long. The illness which had plagued me for several weeks began to increase its hold on my body.

One afternoon in mid-June while working at the baby-sitting co-op, I became so nauseated and consumed with headache pain that I finally collapsed. When I was revived, I had to be taken home. I stumbled in the bathroom and noticed that the whites of my eyes were yellowed. I tried to whiten them with drops to no avail. I took a good look at myself, thin and frail, and saw that my skin was yellowing, too. I called Ron and he came home immediately. He loaded us all into his SUV and took me to the emergency room at the compound hospital. Within minutes, I was ripped from my family and put into total isolation. I had hepatitis.

Isolation in a Saudi Arabian hospital means no TVs in any room, no picture on any wall, not even another woman patient in the whole place! I spent two and a half dreadful weeks of my life in that room. My only salvation was seeing my children whenever the doctor would permit it. God protected them. . .they never got sick.

In the exhaustive heat of one of those terrible nights in isolation, I tossed and turned feverishly in the dark, unable to sleep in spite of the usually prescribed sleeping tablet. No matter how I turned my body, no matter how contortionary my position became in an effort to find comfort, I was unable to relax. I heard myself moan as I twisted every conceivable way to find a restful position. Back and forth until the muscles in my neck were throbbing and my ankles cramped. Something was different. Something began to descend on me. As the minutes passed by I shook as though in a chill, and perspiration covered every part of me. My quiet moaning turned to sobbing and then to a river of helpless tears. I held the bed rails in a vain attempt to control the trembling. It was impossible to breath through the blinding, persistent tears.

Suddenly, a stillness settled in the room. My crying subsided as I came face to face with the reality of the presence of God. I could feel Him near me as if His hand were in mine.

> *"God says, Be quiet and know that I am God."*
> Psalm 46:10

He had come to talk with me. He had come to confront me. He had come to comfort me. He was there.

I don't know how long I lay in solitude and darkness. The tears still flowed, but I was now quiet, motionless and saturated by those tears as they continued to pour out of me. Finally I was able to answer Him. I couldn't express myself more than to whisper: "Dear Lord, Dear Jesus, let me go. I love you, Lord, but I have to do this. . .I must. Please bless my choice. Please, just let me go." I cried from the very depths of me. His gentle reply passed through my spirit over and over again through the heat of those tears and on into the night:

"YOU ARE MY CHILD. . ."

Chapter 12

FOOLISH WOMAN

"A wise woman strengthens her family, but a foolish
woman destroys hers by what she does."
Proverbs 14:1

I was on my own now. Once dismissed from the hospital
I began packing for the trip back to the United States. By
now, everyone knew: my family, Ron's family, Annie and
Bob. There wasn't a life left unshattered. I didn't care. I'd
made my choice and was anxious to start my new life. I
never quit believing it would work out perfectly. I knew that
if anyone could change things, it would be me. I wanted
Craig so much, and I guess I just wanted a change to the
point that I would let nothing stand in my way.

Ron's contract was still current, and he had many months
remaining to fulfill it. I didn't know when he would return
permanently to America. I would think about that later.
Right then the children were mine and he and I would soon
be parting for always.

He drove us back to Jeddah. It was a quiet ride. At least the
tension had loosened its grip because the masquerade was
over. I think we cared enough about each other to make our

final good-bye a peaceful one. There was an undeniable, distinctive severance in our relationship as we said good-bye at the Jeddah airport that night. First he kissed the children, holding back, fighting back any tears. Then he turned to me one last time, put his arms on my shoulders and looked me full in the face in a way he had never done. Trembling, he smiled and kissed me softly. "Good-bye. I wish you the best. Take good care of the children for me." Then he was gone, disappearing in the crowd without turning back.

It was a twenty-three hour flight to San Francisco from that far corner of the world. I was filled with anticipation, determination and what felt like hope. I knew the chance I was taking, but the gamble was worth it to me. I planned to be a winner, but the enemy was planning my ruin.

Satan must have laughed as my anticipation grew. I'm sure his laughter grew louder and haughtier until it was ringing through the corridors of hell. He was consuming me. He'd been waging this battle for quite some time. He gets no greater pleasure than imposing himself where he really has no authority, then manifesting himself there until he looks stronger and more powerful than he actually is. He was about to win a great battle over me, there was no doubt about it. But the war wasn't over yet.

The victory is already ours in Jesus—any situation, every situation. It would be up to me to yield to God, Who had no intention of losing this war for my life. I had no idea what awaited me when that plane touched down. I only thought I knew. The battle continued.

> *"God's Spirit, who is in you, is greater than the devil,*
> *who is in the world."*
> I John 4:4

I was nervous when we depleaned. The children were eager.

Before I knew it, there he was—standing triumphantly just inside the terminal building with a huge bouquet of spectacular roses and a victorious grin on his face! He hugged the children then grabbed me and held me tight for a long time. He was so big and so strong and I felt so wanted. All my fears left me and hope sprung back into me again. Craig took a small box from his pocket, opened it and again placed that beautiful diamond ring on my finger. "Marry me," he said.

The next few days were spent in a whirlwind of quick preparation. We were married almost immediately by a minister who cared for little else than his $50 fee. I felt better, though, because a Justice of the Peace wouldn't have made me feel married. I wanted God involved. Who was I kidding?

It was a lovely warm day in July. The backyard of 'our' new house served as the perfect backdrop for a small wedding. It gloried in its three terraces, hundreds of flowers and fragrant jasmine. Craig's daughter and sons were present and, of course, Lyndsay and Joshua. That was it. I was surprised by Craig's trembling as he was barely able to slip the wedding band on my finger. He wouldn't wear one himself and it hurt me, but I never mentioned it.

A sweet kiss and we were finally husband and wife. I was ecstatic! Craig was silent. I can't even begin to describe what occurred as I thanked the minister and bade him farewell. I didn't know if he was a committed Christian, but said to him, "We appreciate all you've done. Don't you feel God was here with us?" He did not reply. As he turned to leave, a sudden darkness fell over the sky. I quickly returned to my new husband. He had not had the courtesy to escort the minister to his car with me, and there was a strange stillness about him. A frightening chill went through me. He was a different man from that moment.

We went to dinner after the ceremony and Craig got very

drunk—something I had never seen him do. He passed out when we arrived home, and I spent my wedding night crying myself to sleep. The next morning a good friend of Craig's, who had worked hard to get us back together, happened to call very early. He didn't even know I was back in town. They talked business for almost fifteen minutes, but Craig hung up without mentioning my name or that we'd gotten married the day before! He dressed quietly, poured down a cup of coffee and left for work with a hasty good-bye. After crying all night, I cried all day.

> *"Anything I saw and wanted, I got for myself; I did not miss any pleasure I desired. I was pleased with everything I did, and this pleasure was the reward for all my hard work. But then I looked at what I had done, and I thought about all the hard work. Suddenly I realized it was useless, like chasing the wind. There is nothing to gain from anything we do here on earth."*
> Ecclesiastes 2:10-11

I slipped quietly into a state of shock. Another nightmare. I denied what was happening and pretended it wasn't true. Surely I was imagining all this. Craig loved me. He had come after me again and again and had spent thousands of dollars to get me back. No, I was just a nervous bride. Through the following month, my mother and father remained supportive of me, but their words were cautious, strained and fearful. They would tell me how happy they were that I was where I really wanted to be, but continually reminded me that if I needed anything to come to them right away. A panic welled up from deep inside me.

I absorbed myself with the children and their needs in an attempt to compensate for the fact that Craig was spending more and more time away from us. Lyndsay started kindergarten, and I made sure she had the best of everything at all times. Joshua clung to me as never before and I was prepared to keep him happy no matter what it took.

There were many days when I wound up in a heap on the floor of the huge walk-in closet of our bedroom, crying shamefully over the deterioration of my life. As I searched through the array of gorgeous clothes to pick something just right to wear, I would be overcome by the vanity of these riches. I was so empty inside.

> *"Being respected is more important than having great riches. To be well thought of is better than silver or gold."*
> Proverbs 22:1

The shock turned to panic and the panic to quiet desperation.

As I worked madly to hold together the pieces of our lives, trying to keep everyone happy, an inevitability stared me in the face. I needed my car. Annie and Bob had my car. I had to get it, but how? How could I face them?

Craig urged me to make arrangements to get it—buying another was out of the question. He had no concern that it would mean a painful confrontation with Annie and Bob. I anguished over this for days, tired of the turmoil caused by my cowardice. I became defensive. My life was my own! My choices were my own! It wasn't any of Annie and Bob's business to judge. I would simply ask them to sign the title back to me, thank them and drive away. It sounded easy enough. But they were in Los Angeles and I was in San Francisco, and they must hate me by now. They would have lost all respect for me, so the meeting could probably not be a civil one anyway. I'd made my bed, I would have to lie in it. I called their apartment one lonely afternoon, my heart pounding wildly. Bob answered the phone.

"Marsha. We've been expecting to hear from you. Are you alright?"

I had been married for two weeks, but I couldn't bear to tell him.

"I'm doing well, thank you, Bob. I'm sure you know why I'm calling." Neither did I have the courage to discuss my brief stay in Saudi Arabia.

Bob couldn't resist letting me know how he felt about what I'd done: "I guess your theme song must be 'I Left My Heart in San Francisco', huh Marsh?" It was like a knife thrust into my heart. I stammered to keep my composure.

"I need my car, Bob. I'll be in L.A. next Tuesday. May I pick it up then?" He agreed and we made the arrangements in a curt fashion. He hung up and I added the painful conversation to my growing list of hurts, and the suffering mounted.

Craig had it all figured out. He'd been spending more and more time on Mistress lately, sometimes days on end. He wanted to take her south to Newport Beach. I might as well go with him, he said, and I could pick up my car while I was down there and drive home. He saw no need to drive with me, though; he had to get the boat back. As the days went by, however, he changed his mind. He would leave Mistress in Newport Beach for a change of scenery, drive back with me then make arrangements to fly down on weekends and spend time on his boat. He could then make trips back and forth to Catalina Island and do many things he had always wanted to do. I waited anxiously to be invited to share those wonderful things with him, but the invitation never went past the trip to retrieve my car.

Day by day, I became more desperate to please Craig. How could he be slipping through my fingers? What had I done? What about his promises? Before long I saw myself as the one with the problem. I wasn't doing enough for him.

I was giving too much attention to the children. I wasn't a good enough cook. I needed to learn more about boating so I could share his interests more actively. I needed to keep the house spotless and make sure that Mistress and her galley were always clean and well-stocked, even if it meant driving across the Bay in the middle of the day to get it done. I tried new ways to surprise Craig, to do more and more for him in an effort to hold him. He meant so much to me and we had been through so much together. Surely, if I tried a little harder. . .

The children began to take a back seat to Craig in this panic of mine. I needed to hire domestic help so that I could run all of Craig's errands and have someone to watch them all the time. I would be exhausted at the end of a day trying to give them as much of me as possible and struggling to meet Craig's growing demands and needs better than the day before. I was spreading myself dangerously thin and didn't see that I couldn't be everything to everybody all the time. My rubbery emotions were about to snap, but I wouldn't admit defeat.

I looked forward to the trip south aboard Mistress as the honeymoon we had not yet had. It would make the difference! So romantic! It was what Craig wanted, and I was going to make everything perfect for him the whole time, regardless of what it took. I even convinced my mother to take time off work and come out to stay with the children while we were gone. No intrusions. No worries. Just time alone together doing his favorite thing. It would be my favorite thing, too; I'd make it my favorite thing!

> *"Spend time with the wise and you will become wise,*
> *but the friends of fools will suffer."*
> Proverbs 13:20

The cruise was a stark reminder that things were not going as planned. Craig was preoccupied exclusively with Mistress and her needs. I spent my time cleaning, cooking and reading alone to pass the agonizing hours. Occasionally, I would stand behind Craig, watching him navigate the boat quietly, listening to the splashing waves. I wanted so much to say something—to ask him to come spend time doing something together, but I never did. I had become so afraid of him, afraid of rejection. Mistress had again taken first place in his heart and become his excuse to avoid me. She was always such a convenient excuse. When he tended to her he didn't have to work at our relationship. I hated what was happening. When he talked to me, it was always about Mistress or the next boat he would have. It would be even bigger than she.

I had become his slave, not his wife.

I spent days on end shopping alone on Catalina Island while we docked there for our 'vacation' before heading to the mainland to get my car. Craig worked on the boat. I would call Mother and talk with the children. It was my only joy during that time.

D-day arrived. We took the boat to Newport Beach and left her where Craig had previously arranged to do so. He was increasingly nervous and touchy as we neared the time to visit Annie and Bob. He had never met them, but he disliked them fiercely.

A friend of Craig's from Southern California picked us up in Newport Beach and drove us to Annie and Bob's home. They were expecting us, I was sure, because I had confirmed it with them the day before. But I was not expecting the surprise with which I soon found myself faced. How different it all looked as we pulled up to their front door.

Craig refused to get out of the car then, so I went alone. Bob answered the door. He was pleasant to me and seemed genuinely concerned about me and glad to see me. Then I heard voices. I stepped inside and saw a roomful of my friends, Christian friends, who had been close to Ron and me. Annie and Bob had invited them, and we shared a glance of surprise before I found myself caught up in hugs and good wishes from them all. They thought I was alone. What was I going to do? Secretly, I had never been so glad to see anyone! I excused myself momentarily to get Craig. The truth had to come out.

He came in reluctantly as his buddy drove away. I bravely announced that "this is my husband, Craig."

A hush swept the room. For a moment I thought the floor gave way and everyone was sucked into the hole! It was as quiet as death. No one spoke a word. Craig sweat. Annie cried. Someone finally approached Craig to shake his hand and wish us well. Someone said they hoped Craig realized that as Christians they expected marriage to last and that he had better consider his position before the Lord. Someone asked me if I knew what I was doing.

Craig never opened his mouth—not once. My friends were as uncomfortable as we were. They weren't expecting him and he had not been expecting them. When he was asked about his relationship with God, he lost it all, grabbed me, picked up the vehicle title he saw on the dining room table (signed and valid), pulled me outside and into my car. Annie and Bob handed me the keys in silence. The three of us knew what was going through our minds in that last long look at each other. I have never seen them since. I was to miss them as if I had lost a brother and a sister.

The eight-hour drive back to San Francisco was the worst part of the entire ordeal. There wasn't a word spoken between my new husband and me. Nothing would ever be the same again.

Chapter 13

STARK REALITY

> *"Whoever loves money will never have enough money;*
> *Whoever loves wealth will not be satisfied with it.*
> *This is also useless. The more wealth people have, the*
> *more friends they have to help spend it. So what do*
> *people really gain? They gain nothing except*
> *to look at their riches."*
> Ecclesiastes 5:10,11

The stark reality of what was really happening to Craig surfaced more and more as the weeks went by. I was still seeing him through the eyes of a desperately lonely woman in need of acceptance and affection who believed in him and his promises. I continued to give him the benefit of the doubt and to believe that his attitude would change and we would return to our blissful state of fairytale romance. I also continued to repress the truth about where his heart really was. People we knew mutually had more than once warned me that his insatiable appetite for luxury was out of control. Some had even been shocked that he had made a commitment to one woman at the cost of everything he had flaunted for so long. Such was not really the case. The more

I refused to believe this was happening between us, the more it manifest itself.

Resentment toward Craig grew in me subconsciously when I would see that my desperate attempts to please him took me further and further from my children. I just didn't have time for everything! I gave them as much love as I could when I was available to them, but those times became more and more infrequent. The house needed decorating, the gardener had to be supervised, and the list went on.

Before too long, it became evident that I needed someone to stay at the house and help care for Lyndsay and Joshua when I had to be away. I didn't like the idea at all, but it had to be done. This person would have to be very special; I wouldn't trust my kids to just anyone. Didn't I think I was smart! Well, that choice was used to bring someone special into my life.

God is so good. He put a fine woman in my path. Looking from the outside in, Lea had simply answered my ad in the paper. Her sweet and gentle spirit touched me, and I liked her more than anyone I interviewed. Lyndsay and Joshua loved her immediately. She seemed to radiate kindness and graciousness. She was honest and hard-working and I was so glad I had found her! I certainly didn't realize then what a God-send she was. Soon, though, it was evident that she loved the Lord, and she has had a deep and lasting effect on my life.

There were times when I felt Craig was trying his best to make our marriage work, just as I was. I really believe he wanted to live up to his word; he had just lived another way so long and was unable to totally turn in a different direction without intolerable discomfort. Perhaps the new responsibilities he had taken at age fifty-two frightened him into believing that all he had ever worked for was in jeopardy. One thing is very clear to me today: he took every precaution to protect his treasured possessions. I had been a challenge to him, and once the 'conquest' was won, the game was over.

Reality set in, and marriage made him feel like a caged animal. Daily he raged to be set free of his 'prison'.

My naivety was astonishing. I persevered to save my place in his life as I watched it disintegrate in front of me. For comfort, I looked to the children or to my new friendship with Lea. But there was another Comforter who waited patiently for me:

> *"I have seen what they have done, but I will heal them. I will guide them and comfort them and those who felt sad for them. They will all praise me."*
> Isaiah 57:18

Usually, Craig came home about 8 p.m. after a stop at the spa for a swim and a workout. His ravenous appetite would be met and satisfied by a huge dinner I had labored over (being the inept cook that I really am), polite conversation to get through the meal, then his retirement to the television room alone. I would keep the children entertained and clean the kitchen. After baths and story time and prayers, I would tuck them in and hurry up to Craig for a few minutes together, only to be continually ignored. He was either absorbed with television or already asleep. All communication had long since ceased, but the following day the cycle would begin again and I'd try harder than the day before.

At times I saw a glimmer of hope, but it was always fleeting. I remember the big effort Craig made to take the three of us to Lyndsay's school for open house and a big party. She was thrilled, and I was so proud of him. Even Joshua had a good time. The evening was such a good one until Joshua spilled something on the leather upholstery of the Mercedes and Craig's mood changed in a snap. Back to square one.

On daily errands I often drove by a large church in the heart of Burlingame. I noticed the constant activity and the schedule posted in front of the building. I called the church office and learned of a women's group that met weekly for Bible study. I wanted very much to go. I eagerly shared my anticipation with Craig and he told me, "Go if you want to. Maybe you'll make some new friends."

Well, I did go, but found I couldn't handle it well. The women were polite and friendly and the teaching very good. My heart, though, was so laden with guilt and remorse and unworthiness that I felt embarrassed and ashamed to be dirtying their environment with my presence. I believed I had to "clean up my act" before I could ever be part of a group like that again. Those women didn't know what I'd done or been through—they didn't condemn me. They accepted me, but my shame kept me from joining them and accepting myself.

It was Lea who saw me crying one afternoon and urged me to find someone to talk with at the church I had visited . . . someone compassionate to help me out of the darkness back into the Light. Together, we learned about Barbara, a Christian psychologist at the church with a ministry to troubled marriages. God was with me still.

I enthusiastically shared with Craig my desire to counsel with Barbara and asked if he would be interested in learning how he and I could better communicate. I hoped he wouldn't notice my desperate attempt to save our marriage. He must have been struggling as much as I, because he surprisingly agreed to go. I knew there was hope!

We were trapped in a desperate, vicious cycle: Craig had withdrawn from fear, lack of challenge and frustration. I lost the captivating appeal of confidence, sophistication and independence that had drawn him to me. I had become a dependent, whimpering little thing, too eager to please Craig alone. Somehow, somewhere, I'd lost my individuality and self-respect. I didn't like his cowardice and he no longer saw in me the beauty that had drawn him with such magnetic force. We were both moving fast toward opposite ends of a spectrum, and neither of us admitted the truth of it.

Barbara saw at once the tidal wave of destruction toward which we were heading. She was wonderful. I believe she knew all along, but her gentle way of pointing it out helped us to see it for ourselves. She never forced opinions or behavior on us. As a Christian psychologist, God used her to correct me in love. She met with me alone first, then with both of us for several weeks. When she asked me to let her counsel with Craig alone, I got nervous. God loved me so much, and had set into motion the process of drawing me back to Himself. Barbara was there whenever I needed her. Craig's behavior and insensitivity often had me in tears and on the phone with her late at night; I refused to believe what was happening. She comforted me by reminding me of Jesus' love and protection of me and Craig's refusal of that for his own life. As often as I called, she had me remember God's hand in my life. "You are His child," she told me. His own words to me. I remember only great compassion.

"You are His child," would come to me again and again until I recalled that those were God's words to me that night in Saudi when I asked Him to let me go my own way. I was His child. I am His child. He was my Father. He is my Father. Gradually, painfully, I relented. Slowly but ever so surely His love penetrated my life once again. Barbara saw that Craig would make no room in his life for God, and she had to tell me. She saw his plans and knew I'd have to see them for myself to deal with it. As a sister in Christ, she helped me through what happened next. She could because she'd looked ahead and gained my confidence. I wouldn't be able to handle it alone. Her contact with me stayed close.

It was Christmastime again. Lea was pregnant, and her concerned husband asked that she quit her job so she could take better care of herself. Craig and I had been in independent counseling for over two months by this time.

Lyndsay and Joshua and I had grown so close together while the whirlwind went on around us. Ron was coming back to the States for the holidays and they would be joining him.

On December 19, the weather in California was glorious . . .warm and inviting. All city streets were lined in holiday garb and I wished I were as festive and gay. Christmas lights, Christmas trees, jolly Santas, giggling children and busy shoppers. The kids and I were working hard making ornaments for our own tree and dressing the house with the Christmas spirit. I've always fussed at Christmas and spent precious moments instilling its true beauty into my children's hearts. I was glad to know I could again share Jesus with them. It was a step, a small step, but at least in the right direction. I didn't want them to miss the traditions of the season like Santa and his reindeer, but celebrating Jesus' birthday had always been primary before, and I was determined that this year would be no different.

Craig had gone to the boat again. It was Saturday, and I would be meeting Ron at the airport to take the children to him for the holiday. He planned to fly back to the Midwest to be with his family. Craig let me persuade him to take me to Mexico for the holiday since the children would be gone and we would have some time alone to heal our wounded relationship. His reluctance coupled with our fragile situation had me paranoid of what waited in the next turn of events.

It would be the first time I'd seen Ron since leaving Arabia and marrying Craig. Waiting at that airport made me crazy! How would I behave? What would I say? Spaced, that's what I was; a walking case of the shakes. The once confident woman I had prided myself in being had evaporated to a puddle of nervous anxiety. I didn't even know why I was quivering.

Lyndsay and Joshua practically leaped into his strong, fatherly arms. He was just as delighted to see them again. As he walked toward me, I guessed from his inability to speak that he was as nervous as I. It was a difficult afternoon for me. I wanted Ron to know how I respected him for handling himself so maturely during our hard times. It was important to me that he know I valued his fatherhood and his friendship.

I don't think he was impressed as we loaded his baggage into the Mercedes and drove to his hotel. I don't think he believed for a minute that all these 'things' were making me happy, either. He had lived with me for nearly seven years and could still read me like a book.

"How's it going, Marsh?" He had politely turned his attentions momentarily from the children. Did he really care one way or the other?

"I've had my ups and downs," I confessed. "But things are improving." Now I was lying.

"I'm glad." He stared straight in front of himself. The conversation was light, but we were both searching.

He checked into the hotel and I helped him with his bags and the children. They would be spending the night with him before their flight the next day. We both needed to talk just a little, I think.

We tuned in the TV for the kids then turned our attention to each other and some conversation that probably should have gone unsaid. I should have kissed the children good-bye and left at that point, but I didn't want to. I needed Ron, or was I simply using him for comfort?

In an instant, he pushed me down on the bed and playfully bent over me and held my hands down. I saw pain and a great deal of urgency in his eyes. Tears welled up in both of us. He said only one thing before quickly releasing me.

"How the hell did all this happen? What happened to us?" He fought to gain his composure, stood up and began unpacking. I prepared to leave without a word. He looked up. "We'll walk you to your car. Come on, kids."

I hugged my precious children long and hard before saying good-bye. They cried softly.

"I've found a nice church. I've been taking them there whenever I can." I wanted him to know this was still important to me. He changed the subject.

"Are you alright, Marsh? Something's wrong, isn't it? Listen, what would you say if I suddenly asked you to drop everything and run away with me? Oh, I'm sorry. God, that was stupid. Forget it. I didn't mean it. Forget it." He was so embarrassed. I was amazed. If he had given me two more minutes instead of walking away quickly, I might have said yes. He couldn't have meant it anyway, and I had my own life to live now, just as he did.

I waved at Lyndsay and Joshua as I passed them on my way to the freeway and back to paradise. Hot tears burned down my cheeks all the way home.

Later that night after Craig was parked by the TV, I called the hotel to say good-night to the children and to tell Ron not to be concerned about what had happened. What I really wanted to know was how serious he had been. Surely we couldn't really want each other again. . .

Ron answered the phone, and I could tell immediately that being with the children had calmed him, put him at ease and made him forget everything else. He told me about the girl who was flying up from LA just to share the evening with him before he took the children east for Christmas. She was someone I knew, someone he had worked with years ago when we lived in Southern California. They had since struck up a friendship. I was glad for him. He told me that night, though, that her intentions for him were not his intentions for her. I urged him to give it time and not be too hasty to take any action. I knew he needed someone.

Fortunately, Craig and I were leaving for Mexico the next morning or that whole situation might have played with my mind for days. I eagerly put myself into our own trip and tried to forget everything else.

Mazatlan was perfectly lovely. Craig was unsteady—about

as unsteady as his dollars were against foreign currency. I'm sure he wanted to have a good time, though, to relax, but somehow he just couldn't. He certainly tried to keep me happy, but always without him. He kept busy reading financial books and magazines or yachting material he'd brought along and had no interest whatever in swimming or sunning with me. It was easy to give me money to go shopping to keep me occupied. He could congratulate himself for doing me a favor and ridding himself of me at the same time. We ate our meals together, but avoided any discussion of our problems. I wanted to enjoy myself, too, so I was afraid that discussions might blow it all sky high. I took the hint and did my own touring and swimming and sunning. It didn't even move Craig that other men made passes at me when I was constantly seen alone on the beach.

It got old real fast. On Christmas Eve I asked him to take a walk with me on the beach after dinner. It was so beautiful. . . a cruise ship had anchored not far away and its Christmas lights twinkled and glittered like jewels. The music and laughter I could hear made me want to be wrapped in his arms again and dance the evening away. The moon was magnificent and the roar of the surf absolutely intoxicating. I couldn't remember feeling more romantic. We walked. He didn't hold my hand anymore. Tonight he didn't look at me, either. For awhile I thought it was the romance of the moment that had captured him and left him speechless. But it wasn't. I sat down and asked him to sit with me. Still he said nothing at all. After more than an hour by the ocean without a word between us, he got up and went to our room in silence. Any remaining pieces of my heart crumpled to ashes. "Merry Christmas, Darling," I whispered as he disappeared into the darkness. He was asleep when I returned to the room.

Christmas Day. It was five months to the day since we had gotten married. It was Jesus' birthday.

I got up, slipped on my robe and went to sit on the balcony and watch the ocean. I had to confront him. He didn't have the courage to tell me what was causing his insensitive behavior. He had never had the courage to be honest with me. Now I knew that. I wanted to get to the bottom of the problem. Maybe we could deal with it if he would only talk with me. Did Barbara know something I didn't know?

What was going through his mind? What place did I have in his heart? Was there any room left for me at all? Where had I gone wrong, or was it me? If he would just tell me what to do, I'd fix it. Failure was out of the question. I would not allow our relationship to fall apart while I simply sat back and watched. "Help me, Dear Lord," I prayed. Then I took a deep breath and found the strength to go back and face him.

"Merry Christmas," I smiled as I bent down to kiss his cheek. He was awake. I wondered how long he had been laying there deep in thought.

Something was very, very wrong. His eyes were swollen and red. He was shaking. I didn't have to ask him to talk to me. He broke the silence with one short statement:

"I'm sorry, Marsha. I just can't be married anymore."

O, God.

Chapter 14

TEARS WOULDN'T COME

Tension continued to mount between us even though Craig had let his true feelings be known. Now he was drowning in guilt, shame and disgust with himself, and I lived in shock, denial and rejection. The flight back to California from Mexico was the beginning of several weeks of silent battle. We did not sit together on the plane. We never even saw or spoke to each other. There was nothing left to say, and looking at each other frightened him and shattered me.

Denial was the first emotion to work at that time. I refused to believe it was all coming to this. I didn't plan for this—it hadn't so much as crossed my mind. There was no possibility that Craig could not live up to his commitment. He had done so much to have me. We had done so much to have each other. I had sacrificed everything in my life, spilled my blood on the floor, all for a relationship I believed to be solid and infallible. No, I would not accept the possibility that it had all been for nothing! No! Absolutely no way! I would not let myself believe that I'd be left holding the bag and that all the things that were important to me were going to be lost forever. I would fix it. I would just work harder to fix it!

Craig withdrew more into himself daily. He packed most

of his clothes and drove across the Bay to Alameda where he had again docked Mistress and lived in solitude for many weeks. He'd flown again to Southern California to retrieve the yacht because he missed her and wanted to escape to her to deal with himself. He had to have her back, and she again resumed her original place in his life. He rarely called me. When I called him he would often say he just wasn't ready to talk yet. Friends who had wanted to see us together were now calling, wondering how I had let him down and why couldn't I just hang in there? I replied to none of that kind of rhetoric.

I had no one to support me emotionally. My friends from the past had rejected me one by one and I certainly didn't blame them. I felt completely miserable and totally worthless. If this marriage was really going to fail, it meant I was a failure! Then, too, guilt began to bear on me over the pain I'd caused in the lives of so many who loved me—all to see it collapse this way! I didn't want to face anyone because I was too ugly and knew I could never be acceptable again.

Immediately I put a hedge around Lyndsay and Joshua and became absorbed with sheltering them, believing I really could. The three of us in that big house upset me greatly because it echoed the vain attempt to put a family together and served as a constant reminder of failure. I wanted us to have a fresh, new start where the air was not stale with defeat and disaster.

After several weeks of trying to win Craig back, I admitted that I could take it no more, and the children and I moved to an apartment about a mile and a half away. My major concern then was to avoid changing Lyndsay to another school. It would only add to her trauma. Her principal was very supportive. I was able to keep her in the same school, and her teacher helped keep her spirits high with encouragement. Joshua began attending a pre-school at the request of his developmental specialist. He would have nothing but the best care possible, I'd see to that. He needed the stimulation of other children his age. Besides that, I was fast falling into a state of depression that was quickly becoming debilitating.

While the children were in school, I was in bed. It was all I could do to get up, get them breakfast, get them dressed, take them to school and then crawl back under the covers to hide myself. I lost my appetite and the ability to sleep at night and would not leave my bed during the day. The only person I talked to was Barbara. I continued to counsel with her until I couldn't even face her anymore.

Barbara had prayed for me regularly for weeks because she knew this was coming. Craig had confessed to her way before Christmas that he wanted out of the marriage. There were just too many other things more important to him that had been for too long, and he could not live with the additional responsibility like he thought he could. He simply did not want to be responsible for my needs. Barbara was concerned for Craig. She saw him as a lost soul searching for fulfillment in the wrong places and looking for something he'd never find until he realized his own need for Christ. She knew it was best that he leave under those circumstances, and she wanted to help me through the adjustment and on to a new era in my life. She gently and lovingly persuaded me back to counseling when I couldn't bear to go. Barbara helped me see that Craig was a very, very sorry man but was leaving me to protect me from a sad future. He wanted me to have better, and he knew he had to remove himself from the picture to give me that. The only way for him to please himself and me, he felt, was to set me free. Barbara also knew my self-worth would plummet and that I'd have a hard time dealing with the reality of the situation. She prayed that I'd be delivered from the guilt and denial that would surely follow.

Both my parents came to be with me during the next few

weeks as their jobs permitted. When they had to return home, I'd panic, realizing it was me who would have to make it through every day alone again. I began taking pills to help me sleep at night. I could function fairly well as long as someone I trusted was around, but I became a different person when I was alone and had to deal with the truth of where my life was going. I would walk Lyndsay and Joshua to the park or watch TV with them when they were with me, but I could not often take them where there were crowds. Sometimes we would go to a movie where I could sit in the dark and no one could see me. When we needed groceries, I'd run to the store quickly while they were at school and get back fast and go to bed. Headaches plagued me.

Through all this, I could not cry. Tears just wouldn't come. Neither would I or could I look to the future. . .there was none. It was all over for me. I wanted to die, but my children needed me, and I didn't want them to think they had caused me to take my own life—I didn't want them living with that. With them in mind, I struggled through the long, long days. I'd always be disappointed that I had to face another day of nothing but emptiness. Soon I began taking pills during the day, too, but sleep still would not come.

Craig called me once a week or so. He came by occasionally to check on me and ease his conscience. I'd always welcome him because of the loneliness and desperation. Sometimes I'd be in high spirits as I prepared dinner for him, thinking maybe it would win him back and this nightmare would end. But he would come and go without discussing our situation. When he brought me papers from his attorney, I'd fall apart again and make him leave. That's when he began communicating only by letter as I insisted. He begged me to forgive him and not hate him. He was doing me a favor, he would say, because I deserved better than him. I refused to see him yet I very much missed his affection and the great tenderness he had once shown me.

> *"Just as I was with Moses, so I will be with you.*
> *I will not leave you or forget you."*
> Joshua 1:5

I am His child. God never left me. He was drawing me back to Himself. Miraculously He intervened in my tormented life once more.

The managers of our apartment complex were Christians. They befriended me quickly and were immediately defensive of the children as well. Glen was a police sergeant and Janet worked for the airlines. They had no children, so it was easy for them to fall in love with mine. They kept a close watch over my apartment, and Glen soon began to look for Craig to make sure he stayed away from me. They prayed about how to best help me, and God used them in a mighty way. I learned to trust them, my heart softened, and I began to crave Christian fellowship. I could not face God alone, though. For a long time they just loved me and made themselves available to me.

In mid-March I asked Glen and Janet about the church they attended. Maybe I could go with them "if the doctrine were right". I was still so cautious, still hesitant, still 'scared to death'. They prayed I'd be 'scared back to life'!

Now God was able to minister to my spirit again. I received a call from Saudi Arabia. Ron and I had talked when Craig and I separated, and he was concerned for me. He stayed in touch to be sure the children were alright. I also stayed in touch because I wanted his friendship. Did he mean what he said three months before at Christmastime? Were we reaching out to each other again, or was I just desperately lonely? I needed his forgiveness, yet I couldn't forgive myself. I also wanted him to know I would always make sure the children had the best. But this time his call was different. It was curt and to the point.

He would be coming back to the States for R & R in April, and he was going to marry the woman he'd been seeing. He wanted the children for a visit at that time. He gave me the dates and hung up.

A numbness came over me, leaving me temporarily without my faculties. Though I was genuinely happy for him (I knew how much he needed someone), I knew the end had come for me.

Chapter 15

PAIN IS NOT BIGGER THAN GOD

Guilt is a terrible thing. Guilt is crippling. Guilt comes after great loss and is thereby accompanied by the pain that is born of devastation and ruin.

> *"My guilt has overwhelmed me;*
> *like a load it weighs me down."*
> Psalm 38:4

Without confession and repentance, the guilt begins to play its death dance. I believe it to be Satan's greatest tool to render his victim helpless and without hope. Guilt left to fester like an open wound will eventually deteriorate the body. What a triumph for the enemy! If we LET him have his way with the oppression of guilt he lays on us, his victory becomes massive and we often lose the will to go on.

David suffered under the disability of guilt and cried out to God in Psalm 38:

> *"My sores stink and become infected because I was
> foolish. I am bent over and bowed down; I am
> sad all day long. . .I am weak and faint.
> I moan from the pain I feel."*

Out of all I had faced in this ordeal, I now faced the greatest
strain of all. I had been away from the Lord for so long I'd
forgotten the comfort of His presence. When I began living
alone again, Satan saturated me with worthlessness, shame and
the lie that I had certainly committed the unforgivable. It
wasn't long before I lost hope for my life. The slaughter of my
spirit was so complete that I couldn't make a move toward God
because I felt too unclean. Consequently, I longed for the Lord
and missed His presence, but felt I wasn't worthy anymore.

My new friends, Glen and Janet, were then my only source
of encouragement. They didn't force me to discuss what had
happened, they just befriended me and gave me an acceptance
that demonstrated far more than words have ever said. They
loved me and my children and kept a vigilance around us that
slowly began to touch my dying spirit.

The days grew longer as I spent them in bed, staring out
the window, bound by fear. My life was broken. . .how
would I ever fix it? How had it happened? I had no physical
strength to even try to pick up the pieces. My depression
caused many reversals in my habits. I had always taken such
pride in my appearance; now I looked haggard and drab. My
usual good appetite waned and left me thin and frail. The
sparkle in my eyes was gone and the tears I needed to cry
never seemed to surface. The only people I communicated
with besides Lyndsay and Joshua were Glen and Janet.

I dug out my Bible from the bottom of a drawer where it
had been all this time. I couldn't read it, though, as I was
aware that God wanted me to come to Him personally. I
wouldn't find peace until I sought Him alone, by my own

choice. I wouldn't know the comfort of His Word until I went to Him humbly so He could release me from the bondage that had shredded my life. No one could do it for me. The question now was whether or not I'd have the courage to seek Him.

Malachi 2:16 tells us that God hates divorce. He doesn't hate it because it's embarrassing to Him, but because it is never the solution to a troubled marriage—it's the outcome of the trouble and doesn't heal the relationship. Our God deals in answers. Divorce under any circumstances cannot please Him. He wants to keep us from ever experiencing its devastation. He is interested in our going on to a better, more abundant life. Divorce is only allowed because our hearts are so hardened to God because of it (Jesus' own words in Matthew 19:8). Perfect love cannot rejoice in iniquity. Every divorce is the result of a selfish decision. But divorce is not unforgivable. It is a sin, but God can and does forgive it. It is a transgression against His will. The pain that comes from it is indescribable, no matter how friendly we try to make the world think the divorce is. But the pain is NOT bigger than God. Listen to this: the pain is not bigger than God!

> *"The Lord says, 'Come, let us talk about these things.*
> *Though your sins are like scarlet, they can be as white*
> *as snow. Though your sins are deep red,*
> *they can be white like wool."*
> Isaiah 1:18

Two months after Craig said his last good-bye, when I could take it no longer, my parents were ready to have me committed to an "institution" so I could rest and get well. I was ready to admit defeat, but afraid of death. I would miss my babies too much—they needed me. Early in April I pulled myself together and quietly appeared at the church Glen and Janet had recommended. They didn't know I was there. No one knew me and I liked that. I took the children to Sunday School and unobtrusively found a seat in the crowd and pretended to look just as spiritual as everyone else. I hoped no one would see my hands shaking. My ears became deafened to all that was going on around me. My eyes were drawn to the Cross in front of me. A soft voice whispered to me and grew more audible with each moment that passed. I couldn't take my eyes off the Cross. The world seemed to disappear and I was alone with Him. My body was as paralyzed as my gaze at the Cross. Then I heard what He was saying to me. He was calling my name. He was bidding me to come into His presence by calling my name over and over. I couldn't move.

"Marsha. . .Marsha. You are My child."

Did He still love unlovable me? Did He really want me? I was the most unworthy sinner. He kept calling. "Marsha. You are My child." Again, the same words He had spoken to me in Saudi the night I begged Him to let me have my way—to let me go. "You are My child." Without giving me motion, He opened my ears to the voices around me.

The choir sang the words of my Savior, bidding me to come and stand by the waters sheltered by His comfort. They reminded me that He was aware of my longings and would deny me nothing. He had seen me crying so many times and was speaking to my spirit to tell me once again that it was for those very tears that He had freely given His life.

Not caring who heard me, I cried out to Him and collapsed in the tears that had waited so long to come. "Lord, I want to come home!"

Chapter 16

ALREADY CLEAN

Do you have any idea how He moved in my life after I took that step toward Him? Can you imagine how He talked with me, walked with me and comforted me? He touched me through His Spirit by way of His people. . . people I had never met who loved Him and saw that my heart toward Him now had a purity that flooded out of me when I sought forgiveness. Repentance and forgiveness opened the door to people who loved God and responded willingly to His call to minister to me.

> *"The Lord helps those who have been defeated and takes care of those who are in trouble."*
> Psalm 145:14

The most beautiful part of this time of recovery, when I was again experiencing what it means to be held in the arms of a loving God, was the way the family of God reached out to me. Yes, it began my healing process. But more than that, it taught me about love—real love—the kind the world cannot give; unconditional love and total acceptance. The fear of rejection that had plagued me so long left me quickly simply because

95

of the unmerited love of God through His people. I wanted to
one day again be able to give out what was being given to me
so unselfishly.

There was a difficult side to my recovery. Jesus' forgiveness had quickly penetrated my heart—I had experienced it
before and longed for the comfort of it. Forgiving myself was
an entirely different thing. Prayer was still difficult, and I
went through a time when picturing His face and witnessing
His holiness reminded me only of how unclean I thought I
still was. The residue of sin left me feeling dirty. Don't be
deceived, Friend. Satan was still at work. He realized he had
won a battle but had not yet won the war. His fiery darts of
guilt were still being fired.

> *"We have troubles all around us, but we are not
> defeated. We do not know what to do, but we do not
> give up the hope of living. We are persecuted, but God
> does not leave us. We are hurt sometimes, but we are
> not destroyed. We carry the death of Jesus in our
> own bodies so that the life of Jesus can
> also be seen in our bodies."*
> 2 Corinthians 4:8-10

For several months I easily dissolved in tears over what I
had allowed to happen in my life. Shame enveloped me and
subtly permeated the wounded spirit that wanted to know
healing. One moment I would be basking in the love of God
and the next I would be back in depression and crying myself
to sleep at night. I felt I deserved to be punished. As a result,
whenever I would have communication with Ron concerning
the children, anything condemning he might say pushed
every button in my body with worthlessness and degradation.
I was easy prey and I would totally lose it. I couldn't handle
it. I believed I was still unworthy and loathsome. But my God

was working to show me otherwise.

> *"God is working in you to help you want to do and be able to do what pleases him."*
> Philippians 2:18

Because my desire for healing was so strong, I slowly began to see that my feelings of inadequacy were not nearly as strong and only in the way. Slowly is a big word here. I punished myself for a very long time. After months of personal study in the Word of God, more and more honest conversation with Him and much good teaching, I did see the Truth.

If you are suffering with the inability to forgive yourself when you know God has forgiven you, please don't be as stubborn as I and wait so long to see the Truth. I wasted valuable time that could have brought healing so much sooner.

Jesus' work is totally complete. It is perfectly perfect. The cost for your provision has been fully paid. There is no need for penance because Jesus has already paid the price for you! You and I are bought with a price: His blood (1 Corinthians 7:23). You cannot do more than Jesus has already done. I love the story I was taught about this because it finally made me see the light.

Picture yourself at the checkout counter of the grocery store, nervously waiting for the cashier to ring up your final total for the two weeks' worth of food staring you in the face. You grit your teeth through a forced smile and make out the check, and nobody knows it just about cleans out your checking account. Now, you thank the clerk and head to your car. Suddenly you feel guilty. You really didn't pay enough. Everyone was so courteous and you are so grateful that you just have to go back in there and write another check to pay for your groceries again. Maybe you'll feel

better. Who are you kidding?! Who's going to go back there
and pay for those groceries twice?

Penance is never necessary when a believer has turned to
God for forgiveness and knows he has received it. What IS
necessary is repentance.

> *"You are not pleased by sacrifices, or I would give
> them. You don't want burnt offerings. The sacrifice God
> wants is a broken spirit. God, you will not reject a
> heart that is broken and sorry for sin."*
> Psalm 51:16-17

Repentance is TURNING FROM SIN. When Jesus forgave
the woman at the well who had been in adultery by saying to
the legalistic 'religious' people of that time that he who
doesn't have sin in his life should cast the first stone to kill
her, he then turned to her and said:

> *"Woman, where are they? Has no one judged you
> guilty?" She answered, "No one, sir." Then Jesus said,
> "I also don't judge you guilty. You may go now,
> but don't sin any more."*
> John 8:10-11

When we humble ourselves and realize this treasure of
our inheritance, freedom comes and God can begin to lift us
up. I had to respond to God's ability and not my own. I
needed to receive His pardon with thanksgiving, resist the
devil and leave my life of sin.

> *"So if the Son makes you free, you will be truly free."*
> John 8:36

I was glad when I saw the Light. I was reading in John's gospel one day, and this hit me like a ton of bricks:

> *"I am the true vine; my Father is the gardener.*
> *He cuts off every branch of mine that does not produce*
> *fruit. And he trims and cleans every branch that*
> *produces fruit so that it will produce even more fruit.*
> *You are already clean because of the words I have*
> *spoken to you. Remain in me, and I will remain in you.*
> *A branch cannot produce fruit alone but must remain in*
> *the vine. In the same way, you cannot produce fruit*
> *alone but must remain in me."*
> John 15:1-4

I absolutely shouted for joy when it dawned on me! After months of a slow and agonizing recovery, I knew healing had come! Why had it taken me so long to see it? Those many months held much backsliding in my walk with the Lord—subtle little things that hurt me and others because this Truth was one I hadn't yet seen, and it kept me from getting close to the One who had done so much for me. When I saw it, freedom filled my soul. Freedom!

I wanted my relationship with Jesus even more. I was so thankful. Now I knew I had never failed Him, I had only failed myself. Now I see that I can't live by my feelings. I must live life based entirely on what God says about me in His love letter to me: His Word. He says I am free, and that settles that!

Now my whole prayer life changed. I began to praise God and He became my joy! Then I made a pretty lofty request. I've never forgotten it and God obviously has not, either. I asked Him to someday use my experience to help someone else. I told Him I would be willing to do whatever He asked of me to use this situation and what He had done for me to help someone else.

Chapter 17

DREAMING GOD'S DREAMS

> *"All who make themselves great will be made humble,*
> *but all who make themselves humble will be made great."*
> Luke 18:14

My life was devastated. Everything was different now, and never to be the same. I soon would be facing the awful reality of turning my children over to their father because of my contractual agreement with him. Much damage had been done. The wound was deep, but I know God is deeper still. Nothing is too difficult for Him. I rest in Him and He fills me with the assurance that He is repairing the damage that has been done.

> *"But the people who trust the Lord will become strong*
> *again. They will rise up as an eagle in the sky;*
> *they will run and not need rest; they will walk*
> *and not become tired."*
> Isaiah 40:31

Are you still with me, or are you saying to yourself,

"That's no big deal"?

Maybe you live by the philosophy that all things work together for good. Maybe you're even recalling that those words are biblical in origin. Well, you're right. You're absolutely right. But you're not totally enlightened yet. That precious verse of scripture misquoted so much, leads one to believe that all you need is yourself and a little bit of time to work through the setbacks in life. Unfortunately, there's no guarantee in that. When you look at that verse in its entirety, you see there is a condition involved.

> *"We know that in everything God works for the good of those who love him. They are the people he called, because that was his plan."*
> Romans 8:28

What a marvelous promise! This unconditional guarantee is yours when Jesus is Lord of your life! That's the Truth! Nothing else works. You have no other guarantee. Please, come out of the darkness and see that you have no claim to this promise without Him! Only when you love God and are called according to His purpose can you ever be assured of having life to its fullest. Anything less will leave you constantly fearful of the future because it gives you no such guarantee, and fear draws the devil like blood draws sharks! God promises you the abundant life when you make Him Lord of it, and it's against His very nature to break a promise. Don't be deceived. Don't settle for second best any longer.

Before the end of that awful year and its shattered beginnings, I longed to be with my family again before going back to work, something I knew I would soon be forced to do. Now that Ron was remarried and doing so well financially, I thought he could offer the children more than I could at that time. They would have a chance to see the world, receive an incomparable private education and more of a home life than I could give them then. When Ron presented me with those facts, I already knew they were true. With me, they would know nothing but babysitters and a struggling mom deep in the throws of an emotional recovery. With Daddy, they had an opportunity they might never have again. My contract said I did not have to give Ron physical custodianship until he returned permanently to the United States, but I had signed that contract without foresight. Nevertheless, it was signed. The inevitability was still there. With love and courage I agreed to let them go early, as long as Ron lived up to his end of the agreement. I had to trust God that he would.

The children and I traveled to my parents' home for a few months of restorative family living before they were to leave. Miracles began to take place. I had been dreaming God's dreams for my life, and He was about to fulfill them.

> *"Why am I so sad? Why am I so upset? I should put my*
> *hope in God and keep praising him,*
> *my Savior and my God."*
> Psalm 43:5

I had been out of the job market for over eight years. In that time, word processing had emerged and I knew I would need that skill to get the job I wanted. I asked my folks to help me find someone in their hometown from whom I could obtain this training before returning to San Francisco. We searched long and hard. One business school was way too expensive, and another didn't have a class beginning again for several months.

One afternoon Mom called home from work with some news.

"I don't know why I didn't think of this before," she

exclaimed in anticipation.

Her close friend had a grandson who was manager of a computer center in town. Mother had called him and he was more than glad to offer me word processing training at no cost! I could work at his center and teach myself with the manuals. I was thrilled. I wanted to go downtown immediately to meet and thank him and get down to the business of learning. That's what I did. . .and that's how I met John Lenski.

Chapter 18

BECACUSE HE LOVES US

> "*He took me to a safe place. Because he delights in me, he saved me.*"
> Psalm 18:19

It's been years now since my fairytale life began to crumble. Nothing has ever made me as secure as the assurance that my God, the God of Abraham, Isaac and Jacob, Mary, Martha and Paul, the risen and living Lord, knows me better than I do. He's always had a beautiful plan for my life. Many times I've taken detours and changed those plans. In His wisdom and mercy He picks up the pieces and makes a new blueprint. Not only are His mercies fresh and new each day (Lam. 3:23), but they are unending (Matt. 24:35). The unrenewed areas of my mind, trained by my old nature (the one we are all born with) constantly fights my new nature in Christ, and for many years it usually won. I was a Christless Christian, but no more! No more second best for me ever again. He's made His love for me very clear, and I can at last honestly and joyfully tell you that for me there's no turning back! I've decided to follow Jesus, and that means He's Lord of my life, not just a convenient crutch when things don't go my way. He's the ground I walk on! His words are so true:

> *"The thing you should want most is God's kingdom and doing what God wants. Then all these other things you need will be given to you. Enter through the narrow gate. The gate is wide and the road is wide that leads to hell, and many people enter through that gate. But the gate is small and the road is narrow that leads to true life. Only a few people find that road."*
> Matthew 6:33 and 7:13-14

The dream I had growing up is as much a desire for me now as it was years ago. I'm still old-fashioned. My heart's desire is to be a fulfilled wife and mother and whatever else God calls me to do. He knew that all along. I gave up on myself all too often, but He never gave up on me. Today my life is richer and fuller than I can remember it ever having been.

My husband, John, who unselfishly offered to teach me word processing, is God's greatest gift to me (He'll tell you those were the most expensive lessons he ever gave!). It hasn't been easy all the time, and we aren't perfect, but oh how He has manifest Himself in our lives! When John made his commitment to serve the Lord, he was so filled with the Spirit of God that he has become an admirable spiritual leader. I've seen him go through some of the hardest times of his life since I've known him, but he's never lost his vision or ever looked back to that time in his life when Jesus was just a good man he had heard about. He's a fine man of God who encourages and loves me onward and upward in my own walk with Christ. I have watched him take a great deal of abuse for his faith and always come out smiling with never a loss of his integrity. He will not compromise when it comes to the Lord's place in his life, and he is a wonderful example to me. I had never before experienced what it is to be loved as "Christ loved the church and gave Himself for her," which is the commandment to husbands in the Word of God. The joy of the Lord is truly his strength. God knew what kind of man I needed.

As for me, I've put the past behind me as God in His mercy has expected of me. Some may yet see the old Marsha and think that old patterns in my life probably haven't changed. I can't help what others think. My self-worth comes from another Source. The only one to whom I am accountable is the Lord, and I have released it to Him. He sees me as whole and lovely through the eyes of His Son who has made the provision for me. God is faithful! He is so faithful and has promised to complete His work in us until we are with Him face to face.

> *"God began doing a good work in you, and I am sure*
> *he will continue it until it is finished when*
> *Jesus Christ comes again."*
> Philippians 1:6

I'm in partnership with the God of the universe, and I am one proud lady! Humble and proud at the same time! Is that possible? I've humbled myself before Him and am very proud to be His daughter. He's the King of kings, and that makes me a princess; it makes me royalty, and nothing fills my being as fully as that simple fact.

Everything God does is on the basis of His grace, His unmerited favor that cannot be earned! If I had to earn the favor He's given me, I wouldn't be the woman I am today or have the peace He's brought to my life. Perhaps you, right now, have no peace with God and long for it, but can't come or return to Him because your life is too far into the pit—the mess that's accumulated over the years is too confusing to describe, too thorough to dump on God, too embarrassing to talk with Him about. You say you'll come to Jesus when you clean up the mess, huh? Keep in mind:

> *"I tell you the 'right time' is now, and the*
> *'day of salvation' is now."*
> 2 Corinthians 6:2

If you continue in that line of thinking, as I once did, then Jesus died in vain. All He suffered was meaningless then. Or are you saying the price He paid wasn't enough? He loves you where you are, NOW.

> *"The Lord is good, giving protection in times of trouble.*
> *He knows who trusts in him."*
> Nahum 1:7

I can't tell you all my hurts and difficulties have disappeared. We still live in this world and must deal with the results of our sinful and wrongful choices. The Good News is that in Him we can deal with it. Alone we cannot.

I'm a grandmother today, and I still share my beautiful children with their father. It's been the hardest thing I've ever had to do because I don't want them to pay for my mistakes. Many times it is still painful. My rights were nearly taken from me at one time. Here is where God's strength has shown forth. I have finally learned what it means to walk in obedience. The old me says, "God, please don't ask that of me. I don't want to be kind and forgiving. That person hurt me and I want to hurt back." But He constantly reminds me in prayer that no one could ever hurt me enough to create an indebtedness as great as that for which I've been forgiven!

It helps me to see that others need His love, too, and that He manifests that great love through His people. When I follow His direction and flow in the kind of love that has no conditions attached, peace is always restored, my faith grows and I grow.

> *"I may speak in different languages of people or even angels. But if I do not have love, I am only a noisy bell or a crashing cymbal."*
> 1 Corinthians 13:1

I want people to see something else when they look at me besides a pretty face. I want them to see Jesus, and I want them to know Him. I've quit praying that He'll change others to suit me. Now I pray that He'll work on me.

Yes, I created a very difficult situation with respect to my children when I lived in selfishness and am today living with the result of those wrong choices, and it hurts. But God walks through it with me and has answered every prayer I've had concerning Lyndsay and Joshua. During their stay with us one summer not long after my restoration had begun, they both accepted Jesus as their Savior! You can imagine how that blessed me. Together we're under the covenant of Jesus Christ, and as their mother I can rest in that. Each time we spend together strengthens the relationship I was once afraid I'd lose. They are growing strong in the Lord and His presence sustains them constantly. He has provided wisdom to John and I to deal with parenthood, and it has helped both children come out of the worthlessness they lived under over the breakup of their family. Jesus is Lord to them. He says they are priceless in His eyes and is restoring their self-esteem. John and I also benefit from that, so we're all growing. The healing is there and the repair of the damage is in force. That's how faithful God is! That's how loving

God is. He is not a God of confusion. He is the God of the IMPOSSIBLE.

Oh, yes. Just a couple little presents God gave me. I thought you might want to know. Their names are Dayna and Sonya, and what a great joy they are to John and me. God restored motherhood to me and in doing so has told me that He trusts me with these children. I don't intend to fail Him this time.

I thought I'd never be able to serve Him again, that it was all over for me. But today He's anointed me to a ministry to women that is growing and thriving. I can use my talents and interests to His glory teaching and training other women in the Word and how God intends for them to maximize their potential! His restoration is the complete kind of restoration, and nothing else is necessary to build a life.

> *"Forgetting the past and straining toward what is ahead, I keep trying to reach the goal and get the prize for which God called me through Christ to the life above."*
> Philippians 3:13-14

Jesus is a gentleman. He never forces His way into a life. He comes in by invitation only. He has so much to give you, so much waiting for you. Don't take chances with your life anymore. Even if you don't think you deserve any better than you're getting, God's love says you do. You cannot receive that love from Him the way He intended you to have it until you recognize your need. The angels rejoice when someone turns to God and says, "Yes, Lord Jesus, I've sinned. Please come into my life and take it over. I want to dream your dreams. I'm thankful for what you've done for me at the Cross."

After you meet Him, stay close to Him. Get to know Him

and His true nature. I used to think obedience meant giving
up too much, it meant losing what was valuable to me. I've
learned only too well and only so painfully that it's
disobedience that took everything from me. Give it all to
Him—He's already given His all for you.

> *"Obey God and be at peace with him; this is the way to
> happiness. Accept teaching from his mouth, and keep
> his words in your heart. If you return to the Almighty,
> you will be blessed again. So remove evil from your
> house. Throw your gold nuggets into the dust and your
> fine gold among the rocks in the ravines. Then the
> Almighty will be your gold and the best silver for you.
> You will find pleasure in the Almighty, and you will
> look up to him. You will pray to him, and he will hear
> you, and you will keep your promises to him.
> Anything you decide will be done, and light
> will shine on your ways."*
> Job 22:21-22

Life is out there waiting—Eternal life, abundant life! Yes,
YOU CAN HAVE IT ALL.

ABOUT THE AUTHOR

A devoted wife and mother, Marsha Lenski is a woman challenged by and called of God to revitalize and encourage other women in the Body of Christ. She serves as Director of Women's Ministries in her home church in Central Illinois where she challenges others to their destiny in the love of Jesus through regular Personal Touch Meetings, retreats and activities throughout the state. As founder of Beautiful You Ministries, she has developed and taught biblically-based personal development seminars for women and Christian charm courses for young girls in several states since 1985.

If you'd like to share your comments with the author, or if you'd like information about having Marsha minister at your church or conference, you may contact her at:

Heartland Community Church
3253 N. Brush College Road
Decatur, Illinois 62526
(217) 877-9529
Fax: (217) 877-9642

Printed in the United States
22588LVS00002B/88-96